William J. Fay

NEIL POSTMAN

The Disappearance
of Childhood

Neil Postman is a critic, communications theorist, and Chair
of the Department of Communication Arts and Sciences at
New York University. In 1987 he was given the George
Orwell Award for Clarity in Language by the National Coun-
cil of Teachers of English. In 1989 he received the Distinguished Professor Award at New York University. In the
spring of 1991 he was Laurence Lombard Visiting Professor
of the Press and Public Policy at Harvard University. For ten
years he was editor of *Et Cetera*, the journal of General
Semantics. His seventeen previous books include *Teaching
as a Subversive Activity* (with Charles Weingartner), *Amus-
ing Ourselves to Death, Conscientious Objections,* and *Tech-
nopoly.* He is currently writing a book called *Reinventing
Education.*

NEIL POSTMAN

The Disappearance *of* Childhood

VINTAGE BOOKS

A Division of Random House, Inc.

New York

To Shelley

FIRST VINTAGE BOOKS EDITION, AUGUST 1994

Copyright © 1982, 1994 by Neil Postman

All rights reserved under International and Pan-American Copyright Conventions. Published in the United States by Vintage Books, a division of Random House, Inc., New York, and simultaneously in Canada by Random House of Canada Limited, Toronto. Originally published in hardcover in slightly different form by Delacorte Press, New York, in 1982.

Library of Congress Cataloging-in-Publication Data
Postman, Neil.
    The disappearance of childhood/Neil Postman.—1st Vintage Books ed.
        p. cm.
    Originally published: New York: Delacorte Press, 1982. With new preface.
    Includes bibliographical references and index.
    ISBN 0-679-75166-1
    1. Children. 2. Mass media and children. 3. Children and adults.
I. Title.
HQ767.9.P67 1994
305.23—dc20   94-16385
                            CIP

Manufactured in the United States of America

10 9 8 7

Contents

Preface to the Vintage Edition

In preparing myself to write a new preface to this re-publication of
a twelve-year-old book, I reacquainted myself with it in considerable detail. This was not an unpleasant task, since of all the books
I have written, this one has always been my favorite. But I was not
inclined to pamper it. I was especially looking for predictions,
either implied or stated, that have turned out to be wrong. My
intention was to tell the reader that I had made these errors and
then use this edition as an opportunity to correct them. Believe it
or not, I was hoping to find a few important mistakes. The book,
after all, has a rather sad theme, made all the more unpalatable by
the fact that it offers no strong solutions to the problem it raises—
in fact, no solutions at all. If at least some trends toward the disappearance of childhood had been stayed or reversed since the
book was written, I would have been delighted. It would bring no
shame to me or the book to say something I thought would happen
did not; that something I knew to be happening is no longer happening.

As it is, I must let the book stand as I wrote it in the late 1970s
and early 1980s. Of course some of the examples I gave as evidence of the erosion of the line between childhood and adulthood
will be unfamiliar to young readers. They will have to supply their
own, of which there are now many more to choose. More than
more. The examples one would have available today have a kind of
arrogant relevance that I would not have expected a few years ago.

To put it plainly, the book set out to describe where the idea of childhood came from, why it flourished for 350 years, and why it is rapidly disappearing. My re-reading of the book, sad to say, leads me to change nothing of importance in it. What was happening then is happening now. Only worse.

But I have learned something about the subject over the past twelve years that compels me to add something that is not in the book. I would not have believed it could have been in the book. But I am glad to make an amendment here.

Over the past twelve years, many teachers, from elementary school through university, have discussed the arguments and evidence offered in this book with their students. And some of those students have written letters to me expressing their views on the matter. I have been particularly interested in the opinions of students in the fifth and sixth grades, since they are at an age at which children would not only be suffering the effects of an early unwanted adulthood but could talk about them, even reflect on them. Such students also tend to be direct and economical in their style, having not yet been encouraged to use language to conceal their thoughts. For example, a girl named Narielle concluded her short letter by saying that my ideas were "weird." A boy named Jack said, "I think your essay wasn't very good. Childhood doesn't disappear—snap!—like that." Joseph wrote, "Childhood does not disappear because you watch TV, I think childhood is wasted by going to school five days a week. In my opinion, that is too much. Childhood is too precious to go to school more than half a week." Tina wrote, "When you're a kid, you don't really have to worry about responsibility. Kids get to play around more." John wrote, "I think 18 is the correct age for becoming an adult." Patty: "I don't think that if a ten-year-old kid watches an adult show then that kid is never a child again." Andy: "Most kids who watch TV shows know they are not real."

There are, of course, many things to learn from such comments, but their main lesson for me is that children themselves, are a force in preserving childhood. Not a political force, certainly. But a kind of moral force. In these matters, perhaps we can call them a moral majority. Children, it would seem, not only know there is value in being different from adults, but care that a distinction be made; they know, perhaps better than adults, that something terribly important is lost if that distinction is blurred.

I will stand by the theme of the book: American culture is hostile to the idea of childhood. But it is a comforting, even exhilirating thought that children are not.

NEIL POSTMAN
New York City
1994

Introduction

Children are the living messages we send to a time we will not see. From a biological point of view it is inconceivable that any culture will forget that it needs to reproduce itself. But it is quite possible for a culture to exist without a social idea of children. Unlike infancy, childhood is a social artifact, not a biological category. Our genes contain no clear instructions about who is and who is not a child, and the laws of survival do not require that a distinction be made between the world of an adult and the world of a child. In fact, if we take the word *children* to mean a special class of people somewhere between the ages of seven and, say, seventeen, requiring special forms of nurturing and protection, and believed to be qualitatively different from adults, then there is ample evidence that children have existed for less than four hundred years. Indeed, if we use the word *children* in the fullest sense in which the average American understands it, childhood is not much more than one hundred and fifty years old. To take one small example: The custom of celebrating a child's birthday did not exist in America throughout most of the eighteenth century,[1] and, in fact, the precise marking of a child's age in any way is a relatively recent cultural habit, no more than two hundred years old.[2]

To take a more important example: As late as 1890, American high schools enrolled only seven percent of the fourteen-through seventeen-year-old population.[3] Along with many much younger children, the other ninety-three percent worked at adult labor, some of them from sunup to sunset in all of our great cities.

But we must not confuse, at the outset, social facts with social ideas. The idea of childhood is one of the great inventions of the Renaissance. Perhaps its most humane one. Along with science, the nation-state, and religious freedom, childhood as both a social structure and a psychological condition emerged around the sixteenth century and has been refined and nourished into our own times. But like all social artifacts, its continued existence is not inevitable. Indeed, the origin of this book is in my observation that the idea of childhood is disappearing, and at dazzling speed. Part of my task in the pages to come is to display the evidence that this is so, although I suspect most readers will not require much convincing. Wherever I have gone to speak, or whenever I have written, on the subject of the disappearance of childhood, audiences and readers have not only refrained from disputing the point but have eagerly provided me with evidence of it from their own experience. The observation that the dividing line between childhood and adulthood is rapidly eroding is common enough among those who are paying attention, and is even suspected by those who are not. What isn't so well understood is where childhood comes from in the first place and, still less, why it should be disappearing.

I believe I have some intelligible answers to these questions, most of them generated by a series of conjectures about how media of communication affect the socialization process; in particular, how the printing press created childhood and how the electronic media are "disappearing" it. In other words, as I understand what I have written, the main contribution of this book, such as it is, does not reside in the claim that childhood is disappearing but in a theory as to why such a thing should be happening. The book, therefore, is divided into two parts. Part 1 is concerned with showing where the idea of childhood came from; specifically, what were the communication conditions that, at first, made childhood unnecessary, and then made it inevitable. Part 2 puts us in modern times, and tries to show how the shift from Gutenberg's world to Samuel Morse's has made childhood as a social structure difficult to sustain and, in fact, irrelevant.

There is one question of great importance that this book will not address—namely, What can we do about the disappearance of childhood? The reason is that I do not know the answer. I say this with a mixture of relief and dejection. The relief comes from my not having the burden of instructing others on how to live their lives. In all my previous books I have presumed to point to a more effective way of solving one problem or another. Professional educators are, I believe, supposed to do that sort of thing. I had not imagined how pleasant it can be to acknowledge that one's imaginative reach for solutions goes no farther than one's grasp of the problem.

The dejection, of course, comes from the same source. To have to stand and wait as the charm, malleability, innocence, and curiosity of children are degraded and then transmogrified into the lesser features of pseudo-adulthood is painful and embarrassing and, above all, sad. But I have consoled myself with this thought: If one cannot say anything about how we may prevent a social disaster, perhaps one may also serve by trying to understand why it is occurring.

PART 1

The Invention of Childhood

Chapter 1

When There Were No Children

As I write, twelve- and thirteen-year-old girls are among the highest-paid models in America. In advertisements in all the visual media, they are presented to the public in the guise of knowing and sexually enticing adults, entirely comfortable in the milieu of eroticism. After seeing such displays of soft core pornography, those of us not yet fully conditioned to the new American attitudes toward children yearn for the charm and seductive innocence of Lolita.

In cities and towns throughout the country the difference between adult crimes and children's crimes is rapidly narrowing; and in many states the punishments are becoming the same. Between 1950 and 1979 the rate of serious crime committed by those younger than fifteen has increased one hundred and ten times, or eleven thousand percent. Old-timers may wonder about what happened to "juvenile delinquency," and grow nostalgic about a time when a teen-ager who cut class to smoke a cigarette in the school lavatory was considered a "problem."

Old-timers will also remember when there existed an important difference between the clothing of children and adults.

Within the past decade the children's clothing industry has undergone such rapid change that for all practical purposes "children's clothing" has disappeared. It would appear that the idea put forward by Erasmus and then fully accepted in the eighteenth century—namely, that children and adults require different forms of dress—is now rejected by both classes of people.

Like distinctive forms of dress, children's games, once so visible on the streets of our towns and cities, are also disappearing. Even the idea of a children's game seems to be slipping from our grasp. A children's game, as we used to think of it, requires no instructors or umpires or spectators; it uses whatever space and equipment are at hand; it is played for no other reason than pleasure. But Little League baseball and Pee Wee football, for example, not only are supervised by adults but are modeled in every possible way on big league sports. Umpires are needed. Equipment is required. Adults cheer and jeer from the sidelines. It is not pleasure the players are seeking but reputation. Who has seen anyone over the age of nine playing Jacks, Johnny on the Pony, Blindman's Buff, or ball-bouncing rhymes? Peter and Iona Opie, the great English historians of children's games, have identified hundreds of traditional children's games, almost none of which are presently played with any regularity by American children. Even Hide-and-Seek, which was played in Periclean Athens more than two thousand years ago, has now almost completely disappeared from the repertoire of self-organized children's amusements.[1] Children's games, in a phrase, are an endangered species.

As, indeed, is childhood itself. Everywhere one looks, it may be seen that the behavior, language, attitudes, and desires—even the physical appearance—of adults and children are becoming increasingly indistinguishable. No doubt this is why there exists a growing movement to recast the legal rights of children so that they are more or less the same as adults'. (See, for example, Richard Farson's book *Birth-*

rights.) The thrust of this movement, which, among other things, is opposed to compulsory schooling, resides in the claim that what has been thought to be a preferred status for children is instead only an oppression that keeps them from fully participating in society.

I will discuss later the evidence supporting the view that childhood is disappearing, but I want to note here that of all such evidence none is more suggestive than the fact that the history of childhood has now become a major industry among scholars. As if to confirm Marshall McLuhan's observation that when a social artifact becomes obsolete, it is turned into an object of nostalgia and contemplation, historians and social critics have produced, within the past two decades, scores of major works on childhood's history, whereas very few were written between, say, 1800 and 1960.[2] Indeed, it is probably fair to say that Philippe Ariès's *Centuries of Childhood,* published in 1962, created the field and started the rush. Why now? At the very least we may say that the best histories of anything are produced when an event is completed, when a period is waning, when it is unlikely that a new and more robust phase will occur. Historians usually come not to praise but to bury. In any event, they find autopsies easier to do than progress reports.

But even if I am wrong in believing that the sudden preoccupation with recording the history of childhood is, by itself, a sign of the waning of childhood, we can at least be grateful for having available, at long last, accounts of where childhood comes from. Such accounts make it possible for us to learn why an idea like childhood was conceived, and to make conjectures as to why it should become obsolete. What follows, then, is the story of childhood as a careful reader of much of the available material can best piece it together.

Of the attitudes toward children in antiquity, we know very little. The Greeks, for example, paid scant attention to childhood as a special age category, and the old adage that the Greeks had a word for everything does not apply to the concept of a child. Their words for *child* and *youth* are, at the very least, ambiguous, and seem to include almost anyone between infancy and old age. Although none of their paintings have survived, it is unlikely that the Greeks thought it worthwhile to portray children in them. We know, of course, that among their surviving statues, none is of a child.[3]

There are references in their voluminous literature to what we might call children, but these are clouded by ambiguity, so that one cannot get a sure view of the Greek conception, such as it was, of a child. For example, Xenophon tells of the relationship of a man to his young wife. She is not yet fifteen and has been brought up properly "to see as little, and hear as little, and ask as few questions as possible." But since she also reveals that she has been told by her mother that she is of no consequence and that only her husband matters, we cannot clearly judge if we are learning about the Greek attitude toward females or toward children. We do know that among the Greeks as late as Aristotle's time, there were no moral or legal restraints against the practice of infanticide. Although Aristotle believed there should be limits set upon this ghastly tradition, he raised no strong objections to it.[4] From this we may assume that the Greek view of the meaning of a child's life was drastically different from our own. But even this assumption fails on occasion. Herodotus tells several stories that suggest an attitude recognizable to the modern mind. In one such story, ten Corinthians go to a house for the purpose of killing a little boy who, according to an oracle, would grow up to destroy their city. When they arrive at the house, the mother, thinking they are making a friendly visit, places the boy in the arms of one of the men. The boy smiles and, as we would say, captures the hearts of the men, who then leave without performing their dreadful mission. It is not clear how old the boy is, but he is obviously young enough to be held in the arms of an adult. Perhaps if he had been as old as eight or nine, the men would have had no trouble in doing what they came for.

One thing, however, is clear enough. Though the Greeks may have been ambivalent, even confused (by our standards), about the nature of childhood, they were single-mindedly passionate about education. The greatest Athenian philosopher, Plato, wrote extensively on the subject, including no less than three different proposals on how the education of youth ought to be conducted. Moreover, some of his most memorable dialogues are discussions of such questions as whether or not virtue and courage can be taught. (He believed they can.) There can be no doubt that the Greeks invented the idea of school. Their word for it meant "leisure," reflecting a characteristic Athenian belief that at leisure a civilized person would naturally spend his time thinking and learning. Even the ferocious Spartans, who were not strong on what their neighbors would call thinking and learning, established schools. According to Plutarch's life of Lycurgus in the *Lives,* the Spartans enrolled seven-year-old males in classes where they did exercises and played together. They also were taught some reading and writing. "Just enough," Plutarch tells us, "to serve their turn."

As for the Athenians, as is well known, they established a great variety of schools, some of which became vehicles for the spread of Greek culture to many parts of the world. There were their gymnasiums, their ephebic colleges, their schools of the rhetor, and even elementary schools, in which reading and arithmetic were taught. And even though the ages of the young scholars—let us say, at elementary school—were more advanced than we might expect (many Greek boys did not learn to read until adolescence), wherever there are schools, there is consciousness, in some degree, of the specialness of the young.

Nonetheless, the Greek preoccupation with school must not be taken to mean that their conception of childhood parallels our own. Even if we exclude the Spartans, whose methods of discipline, for example, would be regarded by the modern mind as torture, the Greeks did not approach the disciplining of the young with the same measure of empathy and understanding considered normal by moderns. "The evidence which I have collected on methods of disciplining children," notes Lloyd deMause, "leads me to believe that a very large percentage of the children prior to the eighteenth century were what would today be termed 'battered children.' "[5] Indeed, deMause conjectures that a "hundred generations of mothers" impassively watched their infants and children suffer from one source of discomfort or another because the mothers (and, emphatically, the fathers) lacked the psychic mechanism necessary to empathize with children.[6] He is probably correct in this conjecture. There are certainly parents living today who do not have the capacity to empathize with children, and this after four hundred years of child-consciousness. It is, therefore, entirely plausible that when Plato speaks in *Protagoras* of straightening disobedient children by "threats and blows, like a piece of warped wood," we may believe that this is a considerably more primitive version of the traditional warning that if we spare the rod, we will spoil the child. We may also believe that for all their schools, and for all their concern to impart virtue to youth, the ancient Greeks would be mystified by the idea of child psychology or, for that matter, child nurturing.

After saying all of this, I think it fair to conclude that the Greeks gave us a foreshadowing of the idea of childhood. As with so many ideas we take for granted as part of a civilized mentality, we are indebted to the Greeks for this contribution. They did not quite invent childhood, but they came close enough so that two thousand years later, when it *was* invented, we were able to recognize its roots.

The Romans, of course, borrowed the Greek notion of schooling and even developed an awareness of childhood that surpassed the Greek idea. Roman art, for example, reveals "a quite extraordinary sense of age, of the young and growing child, which was not to be found again in Western art until Renaissance times."[7] Moreover, the Romans began to make a connection, taken for granted by moderns, between the growing child and the idea of shame. This was a crucial step in the evolution of the idea of childhood, and I shall have occasion to refer to this connection in discussing the decline of childhood in both medieval Europe and our own times. The point is, simply, that *without a well-developed idea of shame, childhood cannot exist.* To their everlasting credit, the Romans grasped this point, although, apparently, not all of them and not enough of them. In an extraordinary passage in his discussion of education, Quintilian reproaches his peers for their shame-less behavior in the presence of noble Roman children:

> We rejoice if they say something over-free, and words which we should not tolerate from the lips even of an Alexandrian page are greeted with laughter and a kiss. . . . they hear us use such words, they see our mistresses and minions; every dinner party is loud with foul songs, and things are presented to their eyes of which we should blush to speak.[8]

Here we are confronted with an entirely modern view, one that defines childhood, in part, by claiming for it the need to be sheltered from adult secrets, particularly sexual secrets. Quintilian's reproach to adults who neglect to keep these secrets from the young provides a perfect illustration of an attitude that Norbert Elias in his great book *The Civilizing Process* claims as a feature of our civilized culture: that the sexual drive is subjected to strict controls, that great pressure is placed on adults to privatize all their impulses (particularly sexual ones), and that a "conspiracy of silence" concerning sexual urges is maintained in the presence of the young.[9]

Of course, Quintilian was a teacher of oratory and rhetoric, and in the work by which we best know him, he gives an account of how to educate a great orator, beginning in infancy. Thus, we may assume that he was far more advanced than most of his contemporaries in his sensitivity to the special features of the young. Nonetheless, there is a traceable line between the sentiment expressed by Quintilian and the first known law prohibiting infanticide. That law does not come until A.D. 374, three centuries after Quintilian.[10] But it is an extension of the idea that children require protection and nurturing, and schooling, and freedom from adult secrets. And then, after the Romans, all such ideas disappear.

Every educated person knows about the invasions of the northern barbarians, the collapse of the Roman empire, the shrouding of classical culture, and Europe's descent into what is called the Dark and then the Middle Ages. Our textbooks cover the transformation well enough except for four points that are often overlooked and that are particularly relevant to the story of childhood. The first is that literacy disappears. The second is that education disappears. The third is that shame disappears. And the fourth, as a consequence of the other three, is that childhood disappears. To understand that consequence, we must examine in some detail the first three developments.

Why literacy should have disappeared is as deep a mystery as any of the unknowns concerning the millennium that spans the fall of Rome and the invention of the printing press. However, the question becomes approachable if put in a form similar to the way it is posed by Eric Havelock in his *Origins of Western Literacy*. "Why . . . after the fall of Rome," he asks, "did it come about that the use of the Roman alphabet contracted to the point where the general population ceased to read and write so that a previous socialized literacy reverted to a condition of virtual craft literacy, once more reversing history?"[11] What is so useful about Havelock's question is his distinction between "social literacy" and "craft literacy." By social literacy he means a condition where most people can and do read. By craft literacy he means a condition where the art of reading is restricted to a few who form a "scribal" and, therefore, a privileged class. In other words, if we define a literate culture not on the basis of its having a writing system but on the basis of how many people can read it, and how easily, then the question of why literacy declined permits some plausible conjectures.

One of them is given by Havelock himself, who indicates how, during the Dark and Middle Ages, the styles of writing the letters of the alphabet multiplied, the shapes becoming elaborated and disguised. The Europeans, it would appear, forgot that recognition, which was the Greek word for reading, must be swift and automatic if reading is to be a pervasive practice. The shapes of letters must be, so to speak, transparent, for among the marvelous features of alphabetic writing is that once the letters have been learned, one need not think about them. They disappear psychologically, and do not interpose themselves as an object of thought between the reader and his recollection of spoken language. If calligraphy calls attention to itself, or is ambiguous, the essential idea of literacy is lost, or, to be more accurate, is lost to the majority of people. Havelock writes: "Calligraphic virtuosity of any kind fosters craft literacy and is fostered by it, but is the enemy of social literacy. The unlucky careers of both the Greek and Roman versions of the alphabet during the Dark Ages and the Middle Ages sufficiently demonstrate this fact."[12] What happened in Europe—to put it simply—is not that the alphabet disappeared but that the readers' capacities to interpret it disappeared. To quote Havelock again: "Europe, in effect, reverts for a time to a condition of readership analogous to that which obtained in the pre-Greek Mesopotamian cultures."[13]

Still another explanation for the loss of literacy, by no means contradictory to the first, is that the sources of papyrus and parchment became scarce; or if not that, then that the severity of life did not allow for the energy to manufacture them. We know that paper did not come to medieval Europe until the thirteenth century, at which time the Europeans be-

gan at once to manufacture it, not in the time-honored way—
by hand and foot—but by water-powered mills.[14] It is surely
no accident that the beginnings of the great medieval universities and a corresponding renewed interest in literacy co-
incide with the introduction and manufacture of paper. It is,
therefore, quite plausible that the scarcity of writing surfaces
for several hundred years created a situation inimical to social
literacy.

We may also conjecture that the Roman Church was not
insensible to the advantages of craft literacy as a means of
keeping control over a large and diverse population; that is
to say, of keeping control over the ideas, organization, and
loyalties of a large and diverse population. Certainly it would
have been in the interests of the Church to encourage a more
restricted access to literacy, to have its clerics form a scribal
class that alone would have access to theological and intellectual secrets.

But whatever the reasons, there can be no doubt that social
literacy disappeared for close to a thousand years; and nothing can convey better the sense of what that means than the
image of a medieval reader tortuously working on a text.
With few exceptions, medieval readers, regardless of age, did
not and could not read as we do. If such a person could have
seen a modern reader whisk through a page, silently, eyes
rapidly moving, lips in repose, he might have interpreted it as
an act of magic. The typical medieval reader proceeded something like one of our own recalcitrant first graders: word by
word, muttering to himself, pronouncing aloud, finger pointed
at each word, hardly expecting any of it to make much sense.[15]
And here I am referring to those who were scholars. Most
people did not read at all.

What this meant is that all important social interactions
were conducted through oral means, face-to-face. In the
Middle Ages, Barbara Tuchman tells us, "The average layman
acquired knowledge mainly by ear, through public sermons,
mystery plays, and the recital of narrative poems, ballads,

and tales."[16] Thus, Europe returned to a "natural" condition of human communication, dominated by talk and reinforced by song. For almost all of our history, that is the way human beings have conducted their affairs and created culture. After all, as Havelock has reminded us, biologically we are all oralists. Our genes are programmed for spoken language. Literacy, on the other hand, is a product of cultural conditioning.[17] To this, Jean-Jacques Rousseau, the great advocate of the noble savage, would readily agree, and he would add that if men are to live as close to nature as possible, they must despise books and reading. In *Émile* he tells us that "reading is the scourge of childhood, for books teach us to talk about things we know nothing about."

Rousseau is, I believe, correct, if one may take him to mean that reading is the end of *permanent* childhood and that it undermines both the psychology and sociology of oralism. Because reading makes it possible to enter a non-observed and abstract world of knowledge, it creates a split between those who cannot read and those who can. Reading is the scourge of childhood because, in a sense, it creates adulthood. Literature of all kinds—including maps, charts, contracts, and deeds—collects and keeps valuable secrets. Thus, in a literate world to be an adult implies having access to cultural secrets codified in unnatural symbols. In a literate world children must *become* adults. But in a nonliterate world there is no need to distinguish sharply between the child and the adult, for there are few secrets, and the culture does not need to provide training in how to understand itself.

That is why, as Ms. Tuchman also notes, medieval behavior was characterized by childishness among all age groups.[18] In an oral world there is not much of a concept of an adult and, therefore, even less of a child. And that is why, in all the sources, one finds that in the Middle Ages childhood ended at age seven. Why seven? *Because that is the age at which children have command over speech.* They can say and understand what adults can say and understand. They are able to know all the secrets of the tongue, which are the only secrets they need to know. And this helps us to explain why the Catholic Church designated age seven as the age at which one was assumed to know the difference between right and wrong, the age of reason. It also helps us to explain why, until the seventeenth century, the words used to denote young males could refer to men of thirty, forty, or fifty, for there was no word—in French, German, or English—for a young male between the ages of seven and sixteen. The word *child* expressed kinship, not an age.[19] But most of all, the oralism of the Middle Ages helps us to explain why there were no primary schools. For where biology determines communication competence, there is no need for such schools.

Of course, schools are not unknown in the Middle Ages, some of them associated with the Church, some of them private. But the complete absence of the idea of a primary education to teach reading and writing and to provide a foundation for further learning proves the absence of a concept of a literate education. The medieval way of learning is the way of the oralist; it occurs essentially through apprenticeship and service—what we would call "on-the-job training." Such schools as existed were characterized by a "lack of gradation in the curricula according to the difficulty of the subject matter, the simultaneity with which subjects were taught, the mixing of the ages, and the liberty of the pupils."[20] If a medieval child got to school, he would have begun as late as age ten, probably later. He would have lived on his own in lodgings in the town, far from his family. It would have been common for him to find in his class adults of all ages, and he would not have perceived himself as different from them. He certainly would not have found any correspondence between the ages of students and what they studied. There would have been constant repetition in the lectures, since new students were continuously arriving and would not have heard what the Master had said previously. There were, of course, no females present, and as soon as the students were loosed from the discipline of the classroom, they would have been free to do whatever they wished on the outside.

What we can say, then, with certainty, is that in the medieval world there was no conception of child development, no conception of prerequisites or sequential learning, no conception of schooling as a preparation for an adult world. As Ariès sums it up: "Medieval civilization had forgotten the paideia of the ancients and knew nothing as yet of modern education. That is the main point: *It had no idea of education* [italics mine]."[21]

Neither, one must add at once, did it have a concept of shame, at least as a modern would understand it. The idea of shame rests, in part, on secrets, as Quintilian knew. One might say that one of the main differences between an adult and a child is that the adult knows about certain facets of life —its mysteries, its contradictions, its violence, its tragedies — that are not considered suitable for children to know; that are, indeed, shameful to reveal to them indiscriminately. In the modern world, as children move toward adulthood, we reveal these secrets to them, in what we believe to be a psychologically assimilable way. But such an idea is possible only in a culture in which there is a sharp distinction between the adult world and the child's world, and where there are institutions that express that difference. The medieval world made no such distinction and had no such institutions.

Immersed in an oral world, living in the same social sphere as adults, unrestrained by segregating institutions, the medieval child would have had access to almost all of the forms of behavior common to the culture. The seven-year-old male was a man in every respect except for his capacity to make love and war.[22] "Certainly," J. H. Plumb writes, "there was no separate world of childhood. Children shared the same games with adults, the same toys, the same fairy stories. They lived their lives together, never apart. The coarse village festival depicted by Brueghel, showing men and women besotted

with drink, groping for each other with unbridled lust, have
children eating and drinking with the adults."[23]

Brueghel's paintings, in fact, show us two things at once:
the inability and unwillingness of the culture to hide anything from children, which is one part of the idea of shame,
and the absence of what became known in the sixteenth century as civilité, which is the other part. There did not exist a
rich content of formal behavior for youth to learn. How im-
poverished that content was in the Middle Ages may be
difficult for moderns to grasp. Erasmus, writing as late as
1523, gives us a vivid image of a German inn in his *Diversoria:*
There are eighty to ninety people sitting together. They are
of all social classes and all ages. Someone is washing clothes,
which he hangs to dry on the stove. Another is cleaning his
boots on the table. There is a common bowl for washing one's
hands, but the water in it is filthy. The smell of garlic and
other odors is everywhere. Spitting is frequent and unrestricted
as to its destination. Everyone is sweating, for the room is
overheated. Some wipe their noses on their clothing, and do
not turn away when doing it. When the meal is brought in,
each person dips his bread into the general dish, takes a bite,
and dips again. There are no forks. Each takes the meat with
his hands from the same dish, drinks wine from the same
goblet, and sips soup from the same bowl.[24]

In order to understand how people could have endured this
—indeed, not even noticed it—we must understand, as Norbert Elias reminds us, that "such people stood in a different
relationship to one another than we do. And this involves not
only the level of clear, rational consciousness; their emotional
life also had a different structure and character."[25] They did
not, for example, have the same concept of private space as
we do; they were not repelled by certain human odors or
bodily functions; they were not shamed by exposing their
own bodily functions to the gaze of others; they felt no disgust
in making contact with the hands and mouths of others. Considering this, we will not be surprised to know that in the

Middle Ages there is no evidence for toilet training in the earliest months of the infant's life.[26] And we will perhaps expect, as was the case, that there was no reluctance to discuss sexual matters in the presence of children. The idea of concealing sexual drives was alien to adults, and the idea of sheltering children from sexual secrets, unknown. "Everything was permitted in their presence: coarse language, scabrous actions and situations; they had heard everything and seen everything."[27] Indeed, it was common enough in the Middle Ages for adults to take liberties with the sexual organs of children. To the medieval mind such practices were merely ribald amusements. As Ariès remarks: "The practice of playing with children's privy parts formed part of a widespread tradition. . . ."[28] Today, that tradition will get you up to thirty years in prison.

The absence of literacy, the absence of the idea of education, the absence of the idea of shame—these are the reasons why the idea of childhood did not exist in the medieval world. Of course, we must include in the story not only the severity of life but in particular the high rate of mortality among children. In part because of children's inability to survive, adults did not, and could not, have the emotional commitment to them that we accept as normal. The prevailing view was to have many children in the hope that two or three might survive. On these grounds, people obviously could not allow themselves to become too attached to the young. Ariès quotes from a document that records a remark made by the neighbor of a distraught mother of five children. In order to comfort the mother, the neighbor says, "Before they are old enough to bother you, you will have lost half of them, or perhaps all of them."[29]

It is not until the late fourteenth century that children are even mentioned in wills and testaments, an indication that adults did not expect them to be around very long.[30] In fact, probably because of this, in some parts of Europe children were treated as neuter genders. In fourteenth-century Italy, for example, the sex of a child who had died was never re-corded.[31] But I believe it would be a mistake to give too much importance to the high mortality rate of children as a way of explaining the absence of the *idea* of childhood. Half the people who died in London between 1730 and 1779 were under five years of age, and yet, by then, England had already developed the idea of childhood.[32] And that is because, as I shall try to show in the next chapter, a new communication environment began to take form in the sixteenth century as a result of printing and social literacy. The printing press created a new definition of adulthood *based on reading competence*, and, correspondingly, a new conception of childhood *based on reading incompetence*. Prior to the coming of that new environment, infancy ended at seven and adulthood began at once. There was no intervening stage because none was needed. That is why prior to the sixteenth century there were no books on child-rearing, and exceedingly few about women in their role as mothers.[33] That is why the young were part of most ceremonies, including funeral processions, there being no reason to shield them from death. That is why there was no such thing as children's literature. Indeed, in litera-ture "the chief role of children was to die, usually drowned, smothered, or abandoned. . . ."[34] That is why there were no books on pediatrics. And why paintings consistently por-trayed children as miniature adults, for as soon as children abandoned swaddling clothes, they dressed exactly like other men and women of their social class. The language of adults and children was also the same. There are, for example, no references anywhere to children's jargon prior to the seven-teenth century, after which they are numerous.[35] And that is why the majority of children did not go to school, for there was nothing of importance to teach them; most of them were sent away from home to do menial work or serve as appren-tices.

In the medieval world, childhood is, in a word, invisible. Tuchman sums it up this way: "Of all the characteristics in which the medieval age differs from the modern, none is so striking as the comparative absence of interest in children."[36]

And then, without anyone's suspecting it, a goldsmith from Mainz, Germany, with the aid of an old winepress, gave birth to childhood.

Chapter 2

The Printing Press
and the New Adult

It is obvious that for an idea like childhood to come into being, there must be a change in the adult world. And such a change must be not only of a great magnitude but of a special nature. Specifically, it must generate a new definition of adulthood. During the Middle Ages there were several social changes, some important inventions, such as the mechanical clock, and many great events, including the Black Death. But nothing occurred that required that adults should alter their conception of adulthood itself. In the middle of the fifteenth century, however, such an event did occur: the invention of the printing press with movable type. The aim of this chapter is to show how the press created a new symbolic world that required, in its turn, a new conception of adulthood. The new adulthood, by definition, excluded children. And as children were expelled from the adult world it became necessary to find another world for them to inhabit. That other world came to be known as childhood.

There are at least seven cities that claim to be the birthplace of the printing press, each of them designating a different man as the inventor. Such a dispute, all by itself, provides us with an example of one of the most astonishing effects of the printing press: It greatly amplified the quest for fame and individual achievement. "It is no accident," Elizabeth Eisenstein remarks in *The Printing Press As an Agent of Change*, ". . . that printing is the first 'invention' which became entangled in a priority struggle and rival national claims."[1] Why no accident? Because, she suggests, the possibility of having one's words and work fixed forever created a new and pervasive idea of selfhood. The printing press is nothing less than a time-machine, easily as potent and as curious as any one of Mr. H. G. Wells's contraptions. Like the mechanical clock, which was also a great time-machine, the printing press captures, domesticates, and transforms time, and in the process alters humanity's consciousness of itself. But whereas the clock, as Lewis Mumford contends, eliminated Eternity as the measure and focus of human actions, the printing press restored it. Printing links the present with forever. It carries personal identity into realms unknown. With the printing press, forever may be addressed by the voice of an individual, not a social aggregate.

No one knows who invented the stirrup, or the longbow, or the button, or even eyeglasses, because the question of personal accomplishment was very nearly irrelevant in the medieval world. Indeed, prior to the printing press the concept of a writer, in the modern sense, did not exist. What did exist is described in detail by Saint Bonaventura, who tells us that in the thirteenth century there were four ways of making books:

> A man might write the works of others, adding and changing nothing, in which case he is simply called a "scribe." . . . Another writes the work of others with additions which are not his own; and he is called a "compiler." . . . Another writes both others' work and his own, but with others' work in principal place, add-

ing his own for purposes of explanation; and he is called a "commentator." . . . Another writes both his own work and others' but with his own work in principal place adding others' for purposes of confirmation; and such a man should be called an "author." . . .[2]

Saint Bonaventura not only does not speak of an original work in the modern sense but makes it clear that by writing, he is referring in great measure to the actual task of writing the words out, which is why the concept of individual, highly personal authorship could not exist within a scribal tradition. Each writer not only made mistakes in copying a text, but was free to add, subtract, clarify, update, or otherwise reconceive the text as he thought necessary. Even such a cherished document as the Magna Charta, which was read twice a year in every shire in England, was by 1237 the subject of some controversy over which of several versions was authentic.[3]

After printing, the question of who wrote what became important, as did the question of who did what. Posterity became a living idea, and which names could legitimately live there was a matter worth fighting about. As you can infer from the last sentence in Chapter One, I have accommodated an established tradition by settling on Johann Gensfleisch Gutenberg as the inventor of the printing press with movable type, although the earliest dated example of such printing is, in fact, the Mainz Psalter printed by Johann Fust and Peter Shoeffer, two of Gutenberg's partners. But whoever is truly entitled to the claim—Gutenberg, Laurens Coster, Nicolas Jenson, Fust, Shoeffer, et al[4]—this much is clear: When Gutenberg announced that he had manufactured a book "without the help of reed, stylus, or pen but by the wondrous agreement, proportion, and harmony of punches and types . . . ,"[5] he and any other printers could not have known that they constituted an irresistible revolutionary force; that their infernal machines were, so to speak, the typescript on the wall, spelling out the end of the medieval world. Although many scholars have given expression to this fact, Myron Gilmore's statement in *The World of Humanism* sums it up most succinctly: "The invention of printing with movable type brought about the most radical transformation in the conditions of intellectual life in the history of Western civilization. . . . Its effects were sooner or later felt in every department of human activity."[6]

To understand how those effects have a bearing on the invention and growth of childhood, we may take as a guide the teachings of Harold Innis. Innis stressed that changes in communication technology invariably have three kinds of effects: They alter the structure of interests (the things thought about), the character of symbols (the things thought with), and the nature of community (the area in which thoughts develop).[7] To put it as simply as one can, every machine is an idea, or a conglomerate of ideas. But they are not the sort of ideas that lead an inventor to conceive of a machine in the first place. We cannot know, for example, what was in Gutenberg's mind that led him to connect a winepress to book manufacturing, but it is a safe conjecture that he had no intention of amplifying individualism or, for that matter, of undermining the authority of the Catholic Church. There is a sense in which all inventors are, to use Arthur Koestler's word, sleepwalkers. Or perhaps we might call them Frankensteins, and the entire process, the Frankenstein Syndrome: One creates a machine for a particular and limited purpose. But once the machine is built, we discover —sometimes to our horror, usually to our discomfort, always to our surprise—that it has ideas of its own; that it is quite capable not only of changing our habits but, as Innis tried to show, of changing our habits of mind.

A machine may provide us with a new concept of time, as did the mechanical clock. Or of space and scale, as did the telescope. Or of knowledge, as did the alphabet. Or of the possibilities of improving human biology, as did eyeglasses.

To say it in James Carey's bold way: We may find that the structure of our consciousness has been reshaped to parallel the structure of communication,[8] that we have become what we have made.

The effects of technology are always unpredictable. But they are not always inevitable. There are many instances where a "Frankenstein's monster" was created who, upon waking, looked around, judged himself to be in the wrong place at the wrong time, and went back to sleep. In the early part of the eighth century the Anglo-Saxons had the stirrup available but no genius to see its possibilities. The Franks had both the stirrup and Charles Martel's genius, and as a consequence employed the stirrup to create a new means of war, not to mention an entirely new social and economic system, i.e., feudalism.[9] The Chinese and the Koreans (who invented movable metal type prior to Gutenberg) may or may not have had a genius available to see the possibilities of letterpress printing, but what they definitely did not have available were letters—that is, an alphabetic system of writing. Thus, their "monster" returned to its slumber. Why the Aztecs, who invented the wheel, thought its possibilities were exhausted after attaching it to children's toys is still a mystery, but nonetheless another example of the noninevitability of technology's infusing a culture with new ideas.

Lynn White, Jr., in using still another metaphor to make this point, remarks: "As our understanding of the history of technology increases, it becomes clear that a new device merely opens a door; it does not compel one to enter. The acceptance or rejection of an invention, or the extent to which its implications are realized if it is accepted, depends quite as much upon the condition of a society, and upon the imagination of its leaders, as upon the nature of the technological item itself."[10]

In the case of Gutenberg's press, we know, of course, that European culture was ready to receive it. Europe not only had an alphabetic writing system of two thousand years standing but a fairly rich manuscript tradition, which meant that there were important texts waiting to be printed. The Europeans knew how to manufacture paper, which they had been doing for two hundred years. For all of the widespread illiteracy, there did exist scribes who could read and write, and could teach others to do so. The revival of learning in the thirteenth century, and the rediscovery of the wisdom of classical culture, had whetted appetites for books. Then, too, the growth of commerce and the beginnings of the age of exploration generated a need for news, for durable contracts, for deeds, for reliable and standardized maps.

We may say, then, that the intellectual condition of Europe in the mid-fifteenth century made the printing press necessary, which accounts, no doubt, for the fact that so many men in different places were working on the problem at the same time. To use White's metaphor, the printing press opened a door upon which European culture had been anxiously knocking. And when it was finally opened, the entire culture went flying through.

No geniuses were required to discern some of the implications of printing. Within fifty years after the invention of the press more than eight million books had been printed. By 1480 there were presses in a hundred and ten towns in six different countries, fifty presses in Italy alone. By 1482 Venice was the world's printing capital, and Aldus Manutius, a Venetian, was probably the busiest printer in Christendom. The sign outside his shop indicated a flair for the apt pun as well as the state of his business: "If you would speak with Aldus, hurry—time presses." Half of Aldus's employees were Greek exiles or refugees, so that at the time of his death, in 1515, every known Greek author had been translated and printed.[11]

At about the time of Aldus's death the printing press launched the career of the first journalist, the first literary blackmailer, and the first mass-producer of pornography, all in the person of Pietro Aretino.[12] Born of lowly origins and without education, Aretino understood intuitively that the printing press was an instrument of publicity—that is to say, he invented the newspaper, and it is to him we may also ascribe the origin of confessional writing. With few exceptions, e.g., Saint Augustine's *Confessions,* there was no literary tradition of intimate disclosure, no established "voice" or tone by which private thoughts were expressed publicly. Certainly there were no rhetorical conventions for addressing a throng that did not exist except in the imagination.[13] Receiving instruction from no one (for there was none to be had), Aretino rushed ahead in print with a stream of anticlerical obscenities, libelous stories, public accusations, and personal opinion, all of which have become part of our journalistic tradition and are to be found still thriving in the present day. His invention of "yellow" journalism and a style in which to express it made him both rich and famous. He was known in his time as the "scourge of Princes," the Citizen Kane of his day.

If the work of Aretino represents the sordid side of a new literary tradition that addresses a mass but unseen public in intimate terms, then the work of Montaigne represents its more wholesome side. Born in 1533, when Aretino was already forty-one years old, Montaigne invented a style, a form of address, a persona, by which a unique individual could, with assurance and directness, address the unseen living, as well as posterity. Montaigne invented the personal essay, which is to individualism what ballads were to collective consciousness—personal history, as against public history. For all of its modesty, humor, and high intelligence, Montaigne's writing does not celebrate community but celebrates only himself—his uniqueness, his quirks, his prejudices. When, four hundred years, later Norman Mailer wrote *Advertisements for Myself,* he was merely continuing, and giving an apt name to, a tradition established by Montaigne—the writer as self-publicist, and discloser, the writer as individual in opposition to the community. As Marshall McLuhan remarked in his characteristic way, "With print the discovery of the vernacular as a PA system was immediate."[14] He had in mind not only Aretino and Montaigne but especially François Rabelais, who was second to none in his capacity for self-assertion and celebration. He boasted, for example, that his *Gargantua* had sold more copies in two months than the Bible in ten years.[15] For this remark he was denounced as ungodly and blasphemous, the entire episode calling to mind similar denunciations, made more recently, of John Lennon for his remark that The Beatles were more influential than Jesus Christ. The point is that scribal culture had worked against the idea of intellectual property rights and therefore of intellectual individuality. As Elizabeth Eisenstein notes, "The conditions of scribal culture . . . held narcissism in check."[16] Print enabled it to break free.

At the same time as the printing press unleashed a heightened and unabashed self-consciousness in writers, it created a similar attitude in readers. For prior to printing, all human communication occurred in a social context. Even such reading as was done used as its model the oral mode, the reader speaking the words aloud while others followed along.[17] But with the printed book another tradition began: the isolated reader and his private eye. Orality became muted, and the reader and his response became separated from a social context. The reader retired within his own mind, and from the sixteenth century to the present what most readers have required of others is their absence, or, if not that, their silence. In reading, both the writer and reader enter into a conspiracy of sorts against social presence and consciousness. Reading is, in a phrase, an antisocial act.

Thus, at both ends of the process—production and consumption—print created a psychological environment within which the claims of individuality became irresistible. This is not to say that individualism was created by the printing press, only that individualism became a normal and acceptable psychological condition. As Leo Lowenthal remarks, "the prevailing philosophy of human nature since the Renaissance has been based on the conception of each individual as a deviant case whose existence consists very largely in his efforts to assert his personality against the restrictive and levelling claims of society."[18]

Following Innis's lead, i.e., his insight that a new communication technology alters the structure of our interests— we may say, then, that the printing press gave us our selves, as unique individuals, to think and talk about. And this intensified sense of self was the seed that led eventually to the flowering of childhood. Childhood did not, of course, emerge overnight. It took nearly two hundred years to become a seemingly irreversible feature of Western civilization. But it could not have happened without the idea that each individual is important in himself, that a human mind and life in some fundamental sense transcend community. For as the idea of personal identity developed, it followed inexorably that it would be applied to the young as well, so that, for example, by the eighteenth century the acceptance of the inevitability of the death of children (Ariès calls it the concept of "necessary wastage") had largely disappeared. In fact, near the end of the sixteenth century the death of a child began to be represented in various ways on parents' tombs. A macabre fact, perhaps, but indicative of a growing awareness that everyone's life counts.

But individualism alone could not have produced childhood, which requires a compelling basis for separating people into different classes. For that, something else needed to happen. And it did. For want of a better term, I shall call it a "knowledge gap." Within fifty years after printing had been invented, it became obvious that the communication environment of European civilization was dissolving and reconstituting itself along different lines. A sharp division developed between those who could read and those who could not, the latter being restricted to a medieval sensibility and level of interest, the former being propelled into a world of new facts and perceptions. With print, new things to talk about proliferated. And they were all in books, or at least in printed form. Lewis Mumford describes the situation this way: "More than any other device, the printed book released people from the domination of the immediate and the local . . . print made a greater impression than actual events. . . . To exist was to exist in print: the rest of the world tended gradually to become more shadowy. *Learning became book-learning* [italics mine]. . . ."[19]

What sort of information was in books? What things were available to learn? There were, first of all, "how to do it" books: books on metallurgy, botany, linguistics, good manners, and, at long last, pediatrics. *The Boke of Chyldren* by Thomas Phaire, published in 1544, is generally considered to be the first book on pediatrics written by an Englishman. (An Italian, Paolo Bagellardo, published an earlier one in 1498.) In his book, Phaire recommends the use of teething rings, and provides a comprehensive list of "grevious and perilous diseases" of children, including "apostume of the brayne" (probably meningitis), terrible dreams, itching, bloodshot eyes, colic and rumbling of the stomach.[20] Publication of books on pediatrics as well as those on manners is a strong indication that the concept of childhood had already begun to form, less than a century after the printing press. But the point here is that the printing press generated what we call today a "knowledge explosion." To be a fully functioning adult required one to go beyond custom and memory into worlds not previously known about or contemplated. For in addition to the general information, such as was found in "how to" books and assorted guides and manuals, the world of commerce was increasingly made up of printed paper: contracts, deeds, promissory notes, and maps. (Not surprisingly, in an environment in which information was becoming standardized and repeatable, mapmakers began to exclude "Paradise" from their charts on the grounds that its location was too uncertain.[21])

In fact, so much new information, of so many diverse types,

was being generated that bookmakers could no longer use the scribal manuscript as their model of a book. By mid-sixteenth century, printers began to experiment with new formats, among the most important innovation being the use of Arabic numerals to number pages. The first known example of such pagination is Johann Froben's first edition of Erasmus's *New Testament,* printed in 1516. Pagination led inevitably to more accurate indexing, annotation, and cross-referencing, which in turn either led to or was accompanied by innovations in punctuation marks, section heads, paragraphing, title paging, and running heads. By the end of the sixteenth century the machine-made book already had a typographic form and a look—indeed, functions—comparable to books of today. But even earlier in the century printers were concerned with the aesthetics and efficiency of book formats. The printer of Machiavelli's *First Decennale* bitterly complained about a pirated edition of that highly successful book. He described the spurious edition as "a miserable cheapjack . . . badly bound, with no margins, tiny title pages, with no endpapers front or back, crooked type, printer's errors in many places."[22] And this a mere fifty years after the invention of the press.

Here it is worth recalling Harold Innis's principle that new communication technologies not only give us new things to think about but new things to think *with*. The form of the printed book created a new way of organizing content, and in so doing, it promoted a new way of organizing thought. The unyielding linearity of the printed book—the sequential nature of its sentence-by-sentence presentation, its paragraphing, its alphabetized indices, its standardized spelling and grammar—led to the habits of thinking that James Joyce mockingly called ABCED-mindedness, meaning a structure of consciousness that closely parallels the structure of typography. This effect of printing is a point that both Harold Innis and Marshall McLuhan extravagantly asserted; but even such a cautious scholar as Elizabeth Eisenstein believes that the emerging format of books, its particular way of codifying information, "helped to reorder the thought of *all* readers, whatever their profession."[23]

There can be little doubt that the organization of books into chapters and sections came to be the accepted way of organizing a subject: the form in which books presented material became the logic of the discipline. Eisenstein gives an interesting case in point from the field of law. The medieval teacher of the *Corpus Juris* could not demonstrate to either his students or himself how each component of the law was related to the logic of the whole because very few teachers had ever seen the *Corpus Juris* as a whole. But beginning in 1553 a print-oriented generation of legal scholars undertook the task of editing the entire manuscript, including reorganizing its parts, dividing it into coherent sections, and indexing citations. By so doing, they made the ancient compilation entirely accessible, stylistically intelligible, and internally consistent, which is to say, they reinvented the subject.[24] Similarly, as Eisenstein notes, "The mere preparation of differently graded textbooks for teaching varied disciplines encouraged a reassessment of inherited procedures and a rearrangement of approaches to diverse fields."[25] In other words, the availability of different texts on the same subject required that there be consistency in how parts were sequenced; and in determining which things came first and which last, textbook writers were recreating their fields.

At the same time, and inevitably, sixteenth-century editors of books became preoccupied with clarity and logic of organization. "The . . . doctrine that every subject could be treated topically," writes Gerald Strauss, "that the best kind of exposition was that which proceeded by analysis, was enthusiastically adopted by publishers and editors."[26] What they were adopting, of course, was a value as to the best way of organizing one's thinking on a subject. It is a value inherent in the structure of books and typography. But by no means the only one. As calligraphy disappeared, so that there was a loss of idiosyncratic script, the impersonality and repeatability of typescript assumed a certain measure of authority. To this day—and notwithstanding the individuality of authors—there is a tendency to believe what appears in print. Indeed, wherever the mark of a unique individual is absent from the printed page, as in textbooks and encyclopedias, the tendency to regard the printed page as a sacrosanct voice of authority is almost overwhelming.

What is being said here is that typography was by no means a neutral conveyor of information. It led to a reorganization of subjects, an emphasis on logic and clarity, an attitude toward the authority of information. It also led to new perceptions of literary form. Prose and poetry, for example, became distinguished from one another by the way in which words were distributed on the printed page. And, of course, the structure of the printed page as well as the portability and repeatability of the printed book played a decisive role not only in the creation of the essay but also in the creation of what became known as the novel. Many of the earliest novelists were themselves printers, such as Samuel Richardson. And in writing what we might call our first science fiction novel (his *Utopia*), Sir Thomas More worked at every stage with his printer. All of which is to say that we can never underestimate the psychological impact of language's massive migration from the ear to the eye, from speech to typography. To be able to *see* one's own language in such durable, repeatable, and standardized form led to the deepest possible relationship to it. Today, with written language all around us so that we cannot manage our affairs without the capacity to read, it is difficult for us to imagine the wonder and significance of reading in the sixteenth and seventeenth centuries. So powerful—perhaps even magical—was the capacity to read that it could save a man from the gallows. In England, for example, a petty thief who could read a sentence from the Bible merely had his thumbs scarred; one who could not met a different fate. "The said Paul reads, to be branded; the said William does not read, to be hanged." This from the judicial record of the sentencing of two men convicted of robbing the house of the earl of Sussex in 1613.[27]

Print made the vernacular into a mass medium for the first time. This fact had consequences not only for individuals but for nations. There can be little doubt that fixed and visualizable language played an enormous role in the development of nationalism. Indeed, linguistic chauvinism coincides exactly with the development of printing: the idea of a "mother tongue" was a product of typography. And so was the idea of Protestantism. There is no upheaval more directly and uncontestedly associated with printing than the Protestant Reformation. For this assertion we have no better authority than Martin Luther himself, who said of printing that it was "God's highest and extremest act of grace, whereby the business of the Gospel is driven forward." Lutheranism and the book are inseparable. And yet for all of Luther's astuteness in the use of printed pamphlets and books as a means of religious propaganda, even he was surprised on occasion by the unsuspected powers of print. "It is a mystery to me," he wrote in a letter to the Pope, "how my theses . . . were spread to so many places. They were meant exclusively for our academic circle here. . . . They were written in such a language that the common people could hardly understand them." Perhaps Luther would not have been so mystified if he had known of Socrates' warning about writing, as expressed in the *Phaedrus*. "Once a word is written," Socrates said, "it goes rolling all about, comes indifferently among those who understand it and those whom it nowise concerns, and is unaware to whom it should address itself and to whom it should not do so." And Socrates did not have in mind the printed book, which compounds the problem a hundredfold. For surely what Luther overlooked here was the sheer *portability* of printed books. Although his theses were written in academic Latin, they were easily transported throughout Germany and other countries, and printers just as easily had them translated into vernaculars.

Luther, of course, was a great advocate of vernacular printing and exploited the fact that the written word goes rolling all about "unaware to whom it should address itself." He wrote a German edition of the Bible so that the Word of God could reach the largest number of people. It would take us some way off the track to discuss here the many interrelations between print and religious rebellion, but it is necessary to stress the obvious fact that the printing press placed the Word of God on every family's kitchen table, and in a language that could be understood. With God's word so accessible, Christians did not require the papacy to interpret it for them. Or so millions of them came to believe. "Christianity," writes Lawrence Stone, "is a religion of the book, namely the Scriptures, and once this book ceased to be a closely guarded secret fit only to be read by the priests, it generated pressure for the creation of a literate society."[28] The Bible became an instrument to think about, but also an instrument to think *with*. For if ever there was an instance of a medium and a message precisely coinciding in their biases, it is the case of printing and Protestantism. Not only did both reveal the possibilities of individual thought and action, but polyglot versions of the Bible transformed the Word of God as revealed in the medieval Latin Bible into the *words* of God. Through print, God became an Englishman, or a German, or a Frenchman, depending on the vernacular in which His words were revealed. The effect of this was to strengthen the cause of nationalism while weakening the sacred nature of scripture. The eventual replacement of love of God with love of Country, from the eighteenth century to the present, may well be one of the consequences of printing. For the past two centuries, for example, Christians have been inspired to make war almost exclusively in the interests of nationhood; God has been left to fend for Himself.

The replacement of medieval, Aristotelian science by modern science may also be attributed in large measure to the press. Copernicus was born at the end of the fifteenth century, and Andreas Vesalius, Tycho Brahe, Francis Bacon, Galileo,

Johannes Kepler, William Harvey, and Descartes were all born in the sixteenth; that is to say, the foundations of modern science were laid within one hundred years after the invention of the printing press. One may get a sense of how dramatic was the changeover from medieval thought to modern science by contemplating the year 1543. In that year both Copernicus's *De Revolutionibus* and Vesalius's *De Fabrica* appeared, the former reconstituting astronomy, the latter, anatomy. How did the new communication environment produce such an outpouring of scientific discovery and genius?

In the first place, print not only created new methods and sources of data collection but vastly increased communication among scientists on a continent-wide basis. Second, the thrust toward standardization resulted in uniform mathematical symbols, including the replacement of Roman with Arabic numerals. Thus, Galileo could refer to mathematics as the "language of Nature," with assurance that other scientists could speak and understand that language. Moreover, standardization largely eliminated ambiguity in texts and reduced error in diagrams, charts, tables, and maps. By making available repeatable visual aids, print made nature appear more uniform and therefore more accessible.

Printing also led to the popularization of scientific ideas through the use of vernaculars. Although some sixteenth-century scientists—Harvey, for example—insisted on writing in Latin, others, such as Bacon, eagerly employed the vernacular in an effort to convey the new spirit and methods of scientific philosophy. The day of the alchemists' secrets ended. Science became public business. Bacon's *Advancement of Learning,* published in 1605, is the first major scientific tract written in English. A year later, Galileo published a vernacular pamphlet that he apparently printed in his own house. Galileo was not insensible to the power of vernacular printing as a means of self-publicity, and, in fact, used it as a method of establishing his claim as inventor of the telescope. Then, too, printing made available a wide assortment of useful classical texts that medieval scholars were either unaware of or had no access to. In 1570, for example, the first English translation of Euclid became available.

By the end of the sixteenth century, not only Euclid but astronomy, anatomy, and physics were available to anyone who could read. New forms of literature were available. The Bible was available. Commercial documents were available. Practical knowledge about machines and agriculture and medicine was available. During the course of the century an entirely new symbolic environment had been created. That environment filled the world with new information and abstract experience. It required new skills, attitudes, and, especially, a new kind of consciousness. Individuality, an enriched capacity for conceptual thought, intellectual vigor, a belief in the authority of the printed word, a passion for clarity, sequence, and reason—all of this moved into the forefront, as the medieval oral environment receded.

What had happened, simply, was that Literate Man had been created. And in his coming, he left behind the children. For in the medieval world neither the young nor the old could read, and their business was in the here and now, in "the immediate and local," as Mumford put it. That is why there had been no need for the idea of childhood, for everyone shared the same information environment and therefore lived in the same social and intellectual world. But as the printing press played out its hand it became obvious that a new kind of adulthood had been invented. From print onward, adulthood had to be earned. It became a symbolic, not a biological, achievement. From print onward, the young would have to *become* adults, and they would have to do it by learning to read, by entering the world of typography. And in order to accomplish that they would require education. Therefore, European civilization reinvented schools. And by so doing, it made childhood a necessity.

Chapter 3

The Incunabula
of Childhood

The first fifty years of the printing press are called the *incunabula,* literally, the cradle period. By the time print moved out of the cradle, the idea of childhood had moved in, and its own incunabula lasted for some two hundred years. After the sixteenth and seventeenth centuries childhood was acknowledged to *exist,* to be a feature of the natural order of things. Writing of childhood's incunabula, J. H. Plumb notes that "Increasingly, the child became an object of respect, a special creature with a different nature and different needs, which required separation and protection from the adult world."[1] Separation is, of course, the key word. In separating people from one another, we create *classes* of people, of which children are a historic and humane example. But Mr. Plumb has it backward. Children were not separated from the rest of the population because they were believed to have a "different nature and different needs." They were believed to have a different nature and needs because they had been separated from the rest of the population. And they were separated because it became essential in their culture that they learn how to read and write, and how to be the sort of people a print culture required.

Of course, it was not entirely clear at the beginning what reading and writing could or would do to people. As we might expect, the prevailing understandings of the process of becoming literate were naïve, just as today our grasp of the effects of electronic media are naïve. The merchant classes, for example, wanted their children to know their ABC's so that they could handle the paper world of commerce.[2] The Lutherans wanted people who could read both vernacular Bibles and grievances against the Church. Some Catholics saw in books a means of instilling a greater sense of obedience to scripture. The Puritans wanted reading to be the main weapon against "the three great evils of Ignorance, Prophaneness, and Idleness."[3] Some of them got what they bargained for, some much more.

By the mid-sixteenth century the Catholics began to pull back from social literacy, perceiving reading as a disintegrating agent, and eventually prohibited the reading of vernacular Bibles, as well as the works of such writers as Erasmus. Reading became equated with heresy, and the Index followed inexorably. The Protestants, who obviously were partial to heresy of a sort, and who, in addition, hoped literacy would aid in dispelling superstition, continued to exploit the resources of print and carried this attitude with them to the New World. Indeed, it is in Presbyterian Scotland that we find the most intense commitment to a literate education for all. In the First Presbyterian Book of Discipline of 1560, there is, for example, a call for a national system of education, the first such proposal in English history. When the Presbyterians were at the height of their political power, they enacted legislation toward that end (the Act of 1646); and in 1696, after their power was restored, they renewed and strengthened the legislation.[4]

One result of the Catholic defection from print and the Protestant alliance with it was an astonishing reversal of the intellectual geography of European culture. Whereas in the

medieval world the level of cultivation and sensibility was
higher in the Mediterranean countries than in northern Europe,
by the end of the seventeenth century the situation had turned
around. Catholicism remained a religion of the image. It
continued and intensified icon worship, and gave extraordinary
attention to the elaboration of its churches and service. Protestantism developed as a religion of the book, and, as a
consequence, discouraged icon worship and moved toward an
austere symbolism. It was observed by Joseph Kay in the
nineteenth century that to attract the poor to religion, one must
either "adorn the spectacle," as did the Catholics, or "educate
the people," as did the Protestants.[5] While Kay may have a
point about how to attract the poor, we must not overlook
the fact that a reading people develop the capacity to con-
ceptualize at a higher level of abstraction than do the illiterate.
Image-centered and lavishly embellished Catholicism was not
so much an appeal to the poor as an accommodation to a
public, of all levels, still habituated to concrete, iconographic
symbolism. The simplicities of Protestantism emerged as a
natural style for a people whom the book had conditioned to
think more abstractly.

Among other things, what this meant was that childhood
evolved unevenly, for after one has sifted through the historical
complexities, a fairly simple equation emerges: Where literacy
was valued highly and persistently, there were schools, and
where there were schools, the concept of childhood developed
rapidly. That is why childhood emerged sooner and in sharper
outline in the British Isles than anywhere else. As early as
the reign of Henry VIII, William Forrest called for primary
education. At age four, he proposed, children should be sent
to school "to lerne some literature" so that they might understand God's ways.[6] A similar idea was put forward by Thomas
Starkey in his *Dialogue,* which proposed parish schools for all
children under seven.[7] In a relatively short time the English
transformed their society into an island of schools. During the
sixteenth century hundreds of bequests were made by villages

for the establishment of free schools for the elementary instruction of local children.[8] A survey by W. K. Jordan reveals that in 1480 there were 34 schools in England. By 1660, there were 444, a school for every 4,400 people, one school approximately every 12 miles.[9]

There were, in fact, three kinds of schools that developed: the elementary or "petty" schools, which taught the three R's; the free schools, which taught mathematics, English composition, and rhetoric; and grammar schools, which trained the young for universities and Inns of Court by teaching them English grammar and classical linguistics. Shakespeare attended a grammar school in Stratford, and his experience there inspired him to express a famous complaint (for he had probably been required to read Lyly's *Latin Grammar*). In *Henry VI,* Part II, Shakespeare wrote:

> Thou hast most traitorously corrupted the youth of the realm in erecting a grammar-school. . . . It will be proved to thy face that thou hast men about thee that usually talk of a noun, and a verb, and such abominable words as no Christian ear can endure to hear.

But most Englishmen did not agree with Shakespeare that the creation of schools corrupted the youth of the realm. Indeed, the English were not even averse to sending females to school: the free instruction given at Norwich was available to children of either sex. And although it must be understood that schooling was largely a middle- and upper-class preoccupation, there is evidence that even among the poor some women could read.

But, of course, many more men. Of 204 men sentenced to death for a first offense by Middlesex justices between 1612 and 1614, 95 of them pleaded "benefit of clergy," which meant that they could meet the challenge of reading a sentence from the Bible and, therefore, would be spared from the gallows.[10] Professor Lawrence Stone concludes from this that if forty-seven percent of the criminal classes could read, the literacy rate among the total male population must have been much higher. (It is possible, of course, that the "criminal classes" were much cleverer than Professor Stone gives them credit for, and that learning to read was high among their priorities.)

In any case, literacy rates are difficult to pin down. Sir Thomas More guessed that in 1533 over half the population could read an English translation of the Bible. Most scholars agree that this estimate is too high, and have settled on a figure (for males) somewhere around forty percent, by the year 1675. This much, however, is known: In the year 1642 more than 2,000 different pamphlets were published. In 1645 more than 700 newspapers were issued. And between 1640 and 1660 the combined total of both pamphlets and newspapers was 22,000.[11] It is possible that by the mid-seventeenth century "England was at all levels the most literate society the world had ever known."[12] Certainly by the beginning of the seventeenth century its political leaders were literate. And this was apparently the case in France, as well. In England the last illiterate to hold high office was the first earl of Rutland. In France it was the Constable Montmorency.[13] Although the achievement of literacy in France (that is to say, the development of schools) lagged behind that of England, by 1627 there were approximately 40,000 children being educated in France.

What all of this led to was a remarkable change in the social status of the young. Because the school was designed for the preparation of a literate adult, the young came to be perceived not as miniature adults but as something quite different altogether—unformed adults. School learning became identified with the special nature of childhood. "Age groups . . . are organized around institutions," Ariès remarks, and just as in the nineteenth century, adolescence became defined by conscription, in the sixteenth and seventeenth centuries, childhood became defined by school attendance. The word *schoolboy* became synonymous with the word *child*. Ivy Pinchbeck and Margaret Hewitt express it this way:

> Whilst under the traditional system [of apprenticeship], "childhood" effectively ended at the age of seven . . . the effect of organized formal education was to prolong the period during which children were withheld from the demands and responsibilities of the adult world. Childhood was, in fact, becoming far less a biological necessity of no more than fleeting importance; it was emerging for the first time as a formative period of increasing significance.[14]

What is being said here is that *childhood became a description of a level of symbolic achievement*. Infancy ended at the point at which command of speech was achieved. Childhood began with the task of learning how to read. Indeed, the word *child* was frequently used to describe adults who could not read, adults who were regarded as intellectually childish. By the seventeenth century, everyone assumed, as Plumb tells us, that "the processes of a literate education should develop with the developing child: reading should begin about four or five, writing follow, and then gradually more sophisticated subjects should be added. . . . Education [became] tied almost inflexibly to the calendar age of children."[15]

But the tie between education and calendar age took some time to develop. The first attempts to establish classes or grades of students were based on the capacities of students to read, not on their calendar ages.[16] Differentiation by age came later. As Ariès explains, the organization of school classes as a hierarchy of reading competence brought the "realization of the special nature of childhood or youth and of the idea that within that childhood or youth a variety of categories existed."[17] Ariès is expressing here a principle of social perception, alluded to earlier: When a group—any group—is formed on the basis of a single characteristic, it is inevitable that other characteristics will be noticed. What starts out as a category of people who must be taught how to read ends up as a category perceived as unique in multiple dimensions. As childhood itself became a social and intellectual category, stages of childhood became visible. Elizabeth Eisenstein sums up the point: "Newly segregated at schools, receiving special printed materials geared to distinct stages of learning, separate 'peer groups' ultimately emerged, a distinctive 'youth culture' . . . came into being."[18]

What followed from this was inevitable, or so it seems in retrospect. For one thing, the clothing of children became different from that of adults. By the end of the sixteenth century custom required that childhood should have its special costume.[19] The difference in children's dress, as well as the difference in adult perception of children's physical features, is well documented in paintings from the sixteenth century forward, i.e., children are no longer depicted as miniature adults. The language of children began to be differentiated from adult speech. As noted earlier, children's jargon or slang was unknown prior to the seventeenth century. Afterward, it developed rapidly and richly. Books on pediatrics proliferated too. One such book, by Thomas Raynald, was so popular that it went through seven editions before 1600, and continued to be published as late as 1676. Even the simple act of naming children underwent change, reflecting the new status of children. In the Middle Ages it was not uncommon for identical names to be given to all siblings, distinguishing one from the other by birth-order labels. But by the seventeenth century that custom had disappeared, and parents commonly assigned each child a unique name, often determined by parents' expectations of the child.[20] Lagging somewhat behind other developments, children's literature began to appear in 1744, when John Newbery, a London publisher, printed the story of Jack the Giant Killer. By 1780, many professional authors had turned their attention to the production of juvenile literature.[21]

As the form of childhood took shape, the form of the modern family also took shape. The essential event in creating the modern family, as Ariès has emphasized, was the invention and then extension of formal schooling.[22] The social requirement that children be formally educated for long periods led to a reorientation of parents' relationships to their children. Their expectations and responsibilities became more serious and enriched as parents evolved into guardians, custodians, protectors, nurturers, punishers, arbiters of taste and rectitude. Eisenstein provides an additional reason for this evolution: "An unending stream of moralizing literature penetrated the privacy of the home. . . . The 'family' [became] endowed with new educational and religious functions."[23] In other words, with books on every conceivable topic becoming available, not only in school but in the marketplace, parents were forced into the role of educators and theologians, and became preoccupied with the task of making their children into God-fearing, literate adults. The family as educational institution begins with print, not only because the family had to ensure that children received an education at school, but also because it had to provide an auxiliary one at home.

But something else happened to the family that has a bearing on the concept of childhood and that ought not to be neglected. In England, to take the most obvious example, there emerged a visible and growing middle class, people with money and a desire to spend it. According to F.R.H. Du Boulay, here's what they did with it: "They invested it in larger homes, with additional rooms for privacy, in portraits of themselves and their families, and in their children through education and clothing. *The surplus of money made it possible to use children as objects of conspicuous consumption* [italics mine]."[24]

What Du Boulay wants us to take into account here is that an improved economic condition played a role in intensifying consciousness of children and in making them more socially visible. Just as it is well to remember that boys were, in fact, the first class of specialized people, we must also remember that they were the boys of the middle class. Unquestionably, childhood began as a middle-class idea, in part because the middle class could afford it. It took another century before the idea filtered down to the lower classes.

All of these developments were the outward signs of the emergence of a new class of people. They were people who spoke differently from adults, who spent their days differently, dressed differently, learned differently, and, in the end, thought differently. What had happened—the underlying structural change—was that through print and its handmaiden, the school, adults found themselves with unprecedented control over the symbolic environment of the young, and were therefore able and required to set forth the conditions by which a child was to become an adult.

In saying this, I do not mean to imply that adults were always aware of what they were doing or why they were doing it. To a considerable extent developments were dictated by the nature of both books and schools. For example, by writing sequenced textbooks and by organizing school classes according to calendar age, schoolmasters invented, as it were, the stages of childhood. Our notions of what a child can learn or ought to learn, and at what ages, were largely derived from the concept of a sequenced curriculum; that is to say, from the concept of the prerequisite.

"Ever since the sixteenth century," Elizabeth Eisenstein remarks, "memorizing a fixed sequence of discrete letters represented by meaningless symbols and sounds has been the gateway to book learning for all children in the West."[25] Professor Eisenstein is here describing the first step toward adulthood—the mastery of the alphabet—which it was determined ought to occur somewhere between the ages of four and six. But the point is that the mastery of the alphabet and then mastery of all the skills and knowledge that were arranged to follow constituted not merely a curriculum but a definition of child development. By creating a concept of a hierarchy of knowledge and skills, adults invented the structure of child development. In fact, as J. H. Plumb observes, ". . . many of the assumptions that we regard almost as belonging to human nature itself were adopted during this time."[26] And since the school curriculum was entirely designed to accommodate the demands of literacy, it is astonishing that educationists have not widely commented on the relationship between the "nature of childhood" and the biases of print. For example, a child evolves toward adulthood by acquiring the sort of intellect we expect of a good reader: a vigorous sense of individuality, the capacity to think logically and sequentially, the capacity to distance oneself from symbols, the capacity to manipulate high orders of abstraction, the capacity to defer gratification.

And, of course, the capacity for extraordinary feats of self-control. It is sometimes overlooked that book learning is "unnatural" in the sense that it requires of the young a high degree of concentration and sedateness that runs counter to their inclinations. Even before "childhood" existed, the young, we can assume, were apt to be more "squiggly" and energetic than adults. Indeed, one of the several reasons why Philippe Ariès has deplored the invention of childhood is that it tended to restrain the high energy levels of youth. In a world without books and schools, youthful exuberance was given the widest possible field in which to express itself. But in a world of book learning such exuberance needed to be sharply modified. Quietness, immobility, contemplation, precise regulation of bodily functions, became highly valued. That is why, beginning in the sixteenth century, schoolmasters and parents began to impose a rather stringent discipline on children. The natural inclinations of children began to be perceived not only as an impediment to book learning but as an expression of an evil character. Thus, "nature" had to be overcome in the interests of achieving both a satisfactory education and a purified soul. The capacity to control and overcome one's nature became one of the defining characteristics of adulthood and therefore one of the essential purposes of education; for some, *the* essential purpose of education. "The young child which lieth in the cradle is both wayward and full of affections," wrote the Puritans Robert Cleaver and John Dod in their book *A Godly Form of Household Government* in 1621. They went on: "And though his body be but small, yet he hath a [wrongdoing] heart, and is altogether inclined to evil. . . . If this sparkle be suffered to increase, it will rage over and burn down the whole house. For we are changed and become good not by birth but by education."[27]

Notwithstanding Rousseau's influential reaction against this sentiment, centuries of children have been subjected to an education designed to make them "good," that is, to make them suppress their natural energies. Of course, children have never found such a regimen to their liking, and as early as 1597, Shakespeare was able to provide us with a poignant and unforgettable image of the child who knows that school is the crucible of adulthood. In the famous "ages of man" passage in *As You Like It,* Shakespeare speaks of "the whining schoolboy, with his satchel/And shining morning face, creeping like snail/Unwillingly to school."

As self-control became important as an intellectual and theological principle, as well as a characteristic of adulthood, it was accordingly reflected in sexual mores and manners. Among the early and most influential books on the subject of both was Erasmus's *Colloquies*, published in 1516. Its intention was to set forth the manner in which boys must regulate their instinctual life. It is fair, I think, to regard this work as the first widely read secular book that takes as its theme the subject of shame. By our standards it does not quite appear that way, since Erasmus discusses matters that by the eighteenth century were already forbidden material in books for children. For example, he describes a hypothetical encounter between a youth and a prostitute, during which the youth resists the solicitations of the prostitute and instead shows her a pathway to virtue. Erasmus also describes a young man wooing a girl, as well as a woman complaining about her husband's wayward behavior. The book tells the young, in other words, how to regard the problem of sex. At the risk of permanently injuring his reputation, one might say that Erasmus was the Judy Blume of his day. But unlike that popular modern author of widely read books about the sexuality of children, Erasmus's intention was not to reduce a sense of shame but to increase it. Erasmus knew, as did John Locke later, and Freud later still, that even when stripped of its theological connotations, shame is an essential element in the civilizing process. It is the price we pay for our triumphs over our nature. The book and the world of book learning represented an almost unqualified triumph over our animal nature; the requirements of a literate society made a finely honed sense of shame necessary. It is stretching a point only a little to say that print—by separating the message from the messenger, by creating an abstract world of thought, by demanding that body be subordinated to mind, by emphasizing the virtues of contemplation—intensified the belief in the duality of mind and body, which in turn encouraged a contemptuous regard for the body. Print gave us the disembodied mind, but it left us with the problem of how to control the rest of us. Shame was the mechanism by which such control would be managed.

By the end of the sixteenth century there existed a theology of the book, a new and growing commercial system based on print, and a new concept of the family organized around schooling. Taken together, they fiercely promoted the idea of restraint in all matters and of the necessity to make clear distinctions between private and public behavior. "[G]radually," writes Norbert Elias, "does a [strong] association of sexuality with shame and embarrassment, and a corresponding restraint of behavior, spread more or less evenly over the whole of society. And only when the distance between adults and children grows does 'sexual enlightenment' become an 'acute problem.' "[28] Elias is saying here that as the concept of childhood developed, society began to collect a rich content of secrets to be kept from the young: secrets about sexual relations, but also about money, about violence, about illness, about death, about social relations. There even developed language secrets—that is, a store of words not to be spoken in the presence of children.

There is a peculiar irony in this because, on the one hand, the emerging book culture broke up "knowledge monopolies," to use Innis's phrase. It made available theological, political, and academic secrets to a vast public that, previously, had no access to them. But on the other hand, by restricting children to book learning, by subjecting them to the psychology of the book learner and the supervision of schoolmasters and parents, print closed off the world of everyday affairs with which the young had been so familiar in the Middle Ages. Eventually, knowledge of these cultural secrets became one of the distinguishing characteristics of adulthood, so that, until recent times, one of the important differences between the child and the adult has been that adults were in possession of information that was not considered suitable for children to know. As children moved toward adulthood we revealed these secrets to them in stages, culminating in "sexual enlightenment."

That is why, by the end of the sixteenth century, schoolteachers were already refusing to allow children to have access to "indecent books," and punishing children for using obscene language. In addition, they were discouraging children from gambling, which in the Middle Ages had been a favorite pastime of the young.[29] And because children could no longer be expected to know the secrets of adult public behavior, books on manners became commonplace. Erasmus, again, led the field. In his *De Civilitate Morium Puerilium,* he set down for the edification of the young some rules on how to conduct oneself in public. "Turn away when spitting," he says, "lest your saliva fall on someone. If anything purulent falls to the ground, it should be trodden upon, lest it nauseate someone. If you are not at liberty to do this, catch the sputum in a small cloth. It is unmannerly to suck back saliva, as equally are those whom we see spitting at every third word not from necessity but from habit."

As to blowing one's nose, Erasmus insists that "to blow your nose on your hat or clothing is rustic . . . nor is it much more polite to use your hand. . . . It is proper to wipe the nostrils with a handkerchief, and to do this while turning away, *if more honorable people are present* [italics his]."

Erasmus was doing several things at once here. First of all, he was inducing a sense of shame in the young, without which they could not gain entry into adulthood. He was also assigning the young to the status of "barbarian," for as childhood was developing there arose the idea, noted earlier, that children are unformed adults who need to be civilized, who need to be trained in the ways of the adult. As the school book revealed to them the secrets of knowledge, so would the etiquette book reveal the secrets of public deportment. "As Socrates brought philosophy from heaven to earth," Erasmus said of his book, "so I have led philosophy to games and banquets." But Erasmus was not merely revealing adults' secrets to the young. He was also creating such secrets. It is important to know that in his books on public conduct Erasmus was addressing adults as well as children. He was building a concept of adulthood as well as a concept of childhood. We must keep in mind Barbara Tuchman's observations about the childishness of the medieval adult; that is to say, as the book and school created the child, they also created the modern concept of the adult. And when later I shall try to show that in our time childhood is disappearing, I mean to say that inevitably a certain form of adulthood is disappearing as well.

In any case, as childhood and adulthood became increasingly differentiated, each sphere elaborated its own symbolic world, and eventually it came to be accepted that the child did not and could not share the language, the learning, the tastes, the appetites, the social life, of an adult. Indeed, the task of the adult was to prepare the child for the management of the adult's symbolic world. By the 1850s the centuries of childhood had done their work, and everywhere in the Western world childhood was both a social principle and a social fact. The irony, of course, is that no one noticed that at about the same time, the seeds of childhood's end were being planted.

Chapter 4

Childhood's Journey

Before we turn to those changes in our symbolic world that are leading to the disassembling of the idea of childhood, it is necessary to give a brief account of childhood's journey from the seventeenth century forward. When I speak about the disappearance of childhood, I am speaking about the disappearance of an idea. We may deepen our understanding of that idea, not to mention our sense of its loss, if we recall some of the obstacles it has faced and influences that have supported it.

For example, it must not be supposed that childhood sprang full grown from Gutenberg's press and the schoolmaster's class. It is true enough, as I have tried to show, that these were the essential events in childhood's formation in the modern world. But like any idea, especially one of worldwide significance, it has meant different things to different people at different times. As each nation tried to understand it and integrate it into its culture, childhood took on an aspect unique to the economic, religious, and intellectual setting in which it appeared. In some cases it was enriched; in some, neglected; in some, degraded. However, at no point did it disappear, although at times it came close enough.

For example, industrialization as developed in the eighteenth century was a constant and formidable enemy of childhood. In England, literacy, schooling, and childhood developed rapidly until the end of the seventeenth century. But with the growth of large industrial cities and the need for factory and mine workers, the special nature of children was subordinated to their utility as a source of cheap labor. "One effect of industrial capitalism," writes Lawrence Stone, "was . . . to add support for the penal and disciplinary aspects of school, which were seen by some largely as a system to break the will and to condition the child to routinized labour in the factory."[1] True enough, *if* the child was lucky enough to attend a school. For English society was particularly ferocious throughout the eighteenth and part of the nineteenth centuries in its treatment of the children of the poor, who were used to fuel the English industrial machine.

"I'm a trapper in the Gauber Pit, I have to trap without a light, and I'm scared. I go at four and sometimes half-past three in the morning and come out at five and half past. I never go to sleep. Sometimes I sing when I've light, but not in the dark: I dare not sing then." This is a description of a day in the mines by an eight-year-old girl, Sarah Gooder, in the mid-nineteenth century.[2] Sarah's revelations and those of other children led eventually to legislation prohibiting the employment of children in mines—that is to say, children under the age of ten!

Somewhat earlier, in 1814, legislation had been introduced that made stealing a child an indictable offense for the first time in English history. While it had been against the law to strip a stolen child of its clothes, there was no legal retribution for the act of actually stealing a child or for selling the child to beggars. But the law exhibited no such reluctance in exacting penalties for crimes committed *by* children. As late as 1780, children could be convicted for any of the more than two hundred crimes for which the penalty was hanging. A seven-year-old girl was hanged at Norwich for stealing a petticoat, and after the Gordon Riots, several children were publicly hanged. "I never saw boys cry so much," said George Selwyn, a witness to the executions.[3]

In a trial held in 1761, Ann Martin was convicted of putting out the eyes of children with whom she then went begging about the country.[4] She was sentenced to a mere two years in Newgate Prison, and most likely would not have been convicted at all if the children had been her own. Her crime, it would appear, consisted of damaging the property of others.

Volumes have been written, including several by Charles Dickens, that tell of the reign of terror visited upon the children of the poor from the eighteenth century until the mid-nineteenth in England: the workhouses, the penal institutions, the textile mills, the mines, the illiteracy, the lack of schools. I choose the phrase "reign of terror" carefully, because it is important to say that just as the Reign of Terror in France did not and could not destroy the idea of political democracy, the brutal treatment of lower-class children did not and could not destroy the idea of childhood. Happily for the future, the idea was made of sterner stuff than were the children who never benefited from it.

There were several reasons why childhood survived the avarice of industrialized England, and one of them is that the middle and upper classes in England kept the idea alive, nurtured it, and extended it. This fact could not have been of the slightest interest or comfort to Sarah Gooder. But it is of significance to world civilization, and particularly to England. Once they had been introduced, the ideas and assumptions associated with childhood never left England; they were merely blocked from reaching a certain class of people. And although England paid a heavy price for this—for example, by remaining until recent times the most class-conscious society in the Western world—eventually childhood and all that it represents penetrated to the lower classes. After 1840, for example, the growth of elementary education was so rapid

that by the end of the nineteenth century, illiteracy had virtually been eliminated for all classes and for both men and
women.[5]

Childhood was not the sort of idea that could be kept
permanently from all segments of a population. Even if the
English middle and upper classes tried hard to do so—and
they did—childhood's development in other countries would
have heavily influenced the course of events—and it did. Just
as the idea of childhood crossed the Channel from England
to Europe in the seventeenth century, it recrossed it from
Europe in the eighteenth and nineteenth centuries. For example, by the late eighteenth century a causal connection
between lack of education and crime among the young was
taken for granted by most civilized people on the Continent,
and a German visitor to England in 1824 remarked: "England,
in which country alone there are annually executed more human
beings than in several other countries taken together, suffers
two millions of her people to walk about in utter ignorance."[6]
In 1833, *The Edinburgh Review* judged that as far as education was concerned throughout Europe, the English people
were at the bottom of the scale, the Germans at the top.[7] If
not the Germans, then surely the Scots, who by the late
eighteenth century had developed the largest elementary school
system and perhaps the best secondary school system in
Europe. The point is that the invention of childhood was an
idea that crossed all national borders, occasionally being
stopped and discouraged but always continuing on its journey.
And while local conditions affected its aspect and progress,
nothing could cause it to disappear. In France, for example,
opposition to social literacy and education came not from an
inhumane industrial capitalism but from Jesuits who feared
the "protestantization" of their religion and culture. But by
the middle of the nineteenth century, France had caught up
with England in its literacy rate, in its schooling of the young,
and therefore in its regard for the meaning of childhood.

The European-wide movement toward a humane conception

of childhood was due, in part, to a heightened sense of government responsibility for the welfare of children. It is important to take note of this fact because in recent years excessive government intervention in the lives of families has been attacked, and, in my opinion, justifiably so.[8] But in the eighteenth and nineteenth centuries, especially in England and among the poorer classes, adults were not often in a position to develop or display the level of affection and commitment toward children that we would regard as normal. It may well be, as deMause has hypothesized, that many adults simply lacked the psychological mechanism by which they could feel tenderness toward children.[9] It may also be that economic degradation effectively limits such feelings wherever they exist. In any case, it is well known that parents regularly treated their children not only as their private property to do with as they wished, but also as chattels whose well-being was expendable in the interests of family survival. In the eighteenth century the idea that the state had the right to act as a protector of children was both novel and radical. Nonetheless, gradually the total authority of parents was humanely modified, so that all social classes were forced into partnership with government in taking responsibility for child nurturing.

Why government began to assume such responsibility may be explained by reference to several forces, among which was a European-wide spirit of reform and learning. We must remember that the eighteenth century was the century of Goethe, of Voltaire, of Diderot, of Kant, of David Hume, of Edward Gibbon. It was also the century of Locke and Rousseau. We might even say that as far as childhood is concerned, in France the Jesuits were no match for Rousseau, as in England the industrial machine could not withstand the ideas of John Locke. By this I mean that the intellectual climate of the eighteenth century—the Enlightenment, as it is called—helped to nourish and spread the idea of childhood.

Locke, for example, exerted enormous influence on childhood's growth through his remarkable book *Some Thoughts*

Concerning Education, published in 1693. Like Erasmus before him, Locke saw the connections between book learning and childhood, and proposed an education that, while it treated the child as a precious resource, nonetheless demanded rigorous attention to the child's intellectual development and capacity for self-control. Even Locke's enlightened views on the nurturing of physical growth had as their purpose the development of a child's powers of reason. A child must have a vigorous body, he wrote, "so that it may be able to obey and execute the orders of the *mind* [his italics]." Locke also grasped the importance of shame as a means of maintaining the distinction between childhood and adulthood. "Esteem and disgrace are, of all others," he wrote, "the most powerful incentives to the mind, when once it is brought to relish them. If you can get into children a love of credit, and an apprehension of shame and disgrace, you have . . . put into 'em the true principle."

But most of all, Locke furthered the theory of childhood through his well-known idea that at birth the mind is a blank tablet, a tabula rasa. Thus, a heavy responsibility fell to parents and schoolmasters (and then, later, to government) for what is eventually written on the mind. An ignorant, shame-less, undisciplined child represented the failure of adults, not the child. Like Freud's ideas about psychic repression two hundred years later, Locke's tabula rasa created a sense of guilt in parents about their children's development, and provided the psychological and epistemological grounds for making the careful nurturing of children a national priority, at least among the merchant classes who were, so to say, Locke's constituents. And although Locke was no Horace Mann, in that his imagination did not admit of equal schooling for all children, he did propose a program of apprenticeships for the education of poor children whose minds, after all, were as malleable as those of the middle and upper classes.

A second great eighteenth-century intellectual influence on the idea of childhood was, of course, Rousseau. Although I believe Rousseau did not clearly understand why childhood had arisen and how it might be maintained (whereas Locke did), he made two powerful contributions to its development. The first was in his insistence that the child is important in himself, not merely as a means to an end. In this he differed sharply from Locke, who saw the child at every point as a potential citizen and perhaps merchant. Rousseau's idea was not entirely original, for at the time Rousseau was writing, there already existed in France a certain reverence for the charm and value of childhood. Indeed, Rousseau himself quotes an old gentleman who, upon being asked by Louis XV whether he liked the eighteenth century better than the seventeenth, replied, "Sire, I spent my youth in reverence towards the old. I find myself compelled to spend my old age in reverence to the young." But Rousseau's power as a writer and his charismatic personality were so great that most of his followers even refused to believe, as Voltaire and other of his enemies revealed, that Rousseau had abandoned his own children to orphanages. Whatever his personal shortcomings may have been, Rousseau's writings aroused a curiosity about the nature of childhood that persists to the present day. We might fairly say that Friedrich Froebel, Johann Pestalozzi, Maria Montessori, Jean Piaget, Arnold Gesell, and A. S. Neill are all Rousseau's intellectual heirs. (Froebel and Pestalozzi explicitly proclaimed their debt.) Certainly their work proceeded from the assumption that the psychology of childhood is fundamentally different from that of adults, and is to be valued for itself.

Rousseau's second idea was that a child's intellectual and emotional life is important, not because we must know about it in order to teach and train our children, but because childhood is the stage of life when man most closely approximates to the "state of nature." Rousseau valued such a state to a degree that no one has since approached, including his intellectual heirs. In *Émile,* his famous book about the ideal education of a child, Rousseau allows only one book to be read by children: *Robinson Crusoe*. And this only because the book demonstrates how man may live in and control a "natural environment." Rousseau's obsession with a state of nature and his corresponding contempt for "civilized values" brought to the world's attention, as no one had done before him, the childhood virtues of spontaneity, purity, strength, and joy, all of which came to be seen as features to nurture and celebrate. And the great artists of the Romantic movement did not fail to take up the "joie de vivre" of childhood as a theme. Wordsworth's poetry in particular depicts adults as "fallen children" and celebrates childhood innocence and naturalness. Wagner's *Siegfried* is often cited (for example, by Ariès) as the most powerful expression of the virtues of adolescence.[10] And it is in the eighteenth century, we should remember, that Gainsborough painted the most romantic and charming picture of adolescence that has ever been done, his "Blue Boy."

And so as childhood moved into the nineteenth and twentieth centuries, and as it crossed the Atlantic to the New World, there were two intellectual strains of which the idea was composed. We might call them the Lockean, or the Protestant, conception of childhood, and the Rousseauian, or the Romantic, conception. In the Protestant view the child is an unformed person who through literacy, education, reason, self-control, and shame may be made into a civilized adult. In the Romantic view it is not the unformed child but the deformed adult who is the problem. The child possesses as his or her birthright capacities for candor, understanding, curiosity, and spontaneity that are deadened by literacy, education, reason, self-control, and shame.

The difference between these two views can be seen most vividly by attending to the contrasting metaphors of childhood put forward by Locke and Rousseau. I do not believe it has been much remarked, for example, that Locke's metaphor of the mind as a tablet depicts precisely the connection between childhood and print. Indeed, the tabula rasa sees the child as an inadequately written book, advancing toward maturity as the pages are filled. There is nothing "natural" or biological about this process. It is a process of symbolic development —sequential, segmented, linguistic. To Locke and most eighteenth-century thinkers, illiteracy and childhood were inseparable, adulthood being defined as total linguistic competence.

On the other hand, Rousseau wrote in *Émile* that "plants are improved by cultivation, and man by education." Here is the child as a wild plant, which can hardly be improved by book learning. Its growth is organic and natural; childhood requires only that it not be suffocated by civilization's diseased outpourings. To Rousseau, education was essentially a subtraction process; to Locke, an addition process. But whatever the differences between these two metaphors, they do have in common a concern for the future. Locke wanted education to result in a rich, varied, and copious book; Rousseau wanted education to result in a healthy flower. This is important to keep in mind, for a concern for the future is increasingly missing from the metaphors of childhood in the present day. Neither Locke nor Rousseau ever doubted that childhood could exist without the future-oriented guidance of adults.

In America, of course, the Protestant view dominated throughout much of the nineteenth century, although the Romantic view was never completely absent. Indeed, we might say that America's greatest book, *The Adventures of Huckleberry Finn*, published in 1884, presents the case for the Romantic view, in spite of the book's somewhat ambiguous ending. Certainly Twain attacked the presumption that children are, in any but the most superficial sense, unformed. And he mocked the claim that their character may be vastly improved by society's "values." Huck's innate sense of fairness and dignity, his resourcefulness and psychological strength, his sheer *interest* in life—all of this struck a blow for the Romantic vision of childhood and was part of a general trend, beginning around the Civil War, toward a reassessment of the nature of childhood. As Lawrence Cremin has shown in *The Transformation of the School*, the origins of the progressive education movement go back to this era. In 1857, for example, what eventually became known as the National Education Association was founded, and in 1875, a charter was issued to the New York Society for the Prevention of Cruelty to Children.[11] (As a matter of ironic contrast, we may ponder the fact that the American Society for the Prevention of Cruelty to Animals was founded nearly a decade earlier, in 1866.)

I do not mean to give the impression here, Huck Finn notwithstanding, that the Lockean view began to fall into disrepute, although this was probably the case for its more extreme Calvinist expression, i.e., that children are depraved. The tradition of Locke, after all, speaks for a high degree of caring and nurturing of children, and, above all, for the linguistic education of children. To this day, in America and throughout Europe, the assumptions of Locke are reflected not only in schools but in most of the institutions concerned with children. But what appears to have happened is that the *certainty* of opinion about the nature of childhood began to be questioned. In general, the Lockean view that children were unformed adults in need of civilizing remained intact, but questions arose as to how to proceed so as not to impair such childhood virtues as were depicted by Rousseau and the Romantic movement. In 1890, for example, the Society for the Study of Child Nature was established, and among the questions that were addressed at its meetings were the following:

Should implicit obedience be enforced upon children?

How can the true idea of property be conveyed to the child?

How much authority should older children have?

Is a child's imagination stunted if it is made to adhere strictly to the truth?[12]

The people who posed such questions were obviously no disciples of Rousseau, although just as obviously they did not wish the process of education to interfere with children's growth; that is to say, they accepted the idea that there is both a logic and psychologic to childhood that must be respected.

Thus, at the end of the nineteenth century, the stage was set for two men whose work eventually established the mode of discourse to be used in all discussions of childhood in the present century. It is worth noting that the most influential book of each man was published in 1899, and each, in its way, led thoughtful people to pose the question: How do we balance the claims of civilization against the claims of a child's nature? I refer, of course, to Sigmund Freud's *The Interpretation of Dreams* and John Dewey's *The School and Society*. Both men and their work are too well known to require much explication, but this much must be said: Taken together, they represent a synthesis and summation of childhood's journey from the sixteenth century to the twentieth.

From within a framework of science Freud claimed, first of all, that there is an undeniable structure, as well as a special content, to the mind of the child—e.g., that children possess sexuality and are imbued with complexes and instinctive psychic drives. He also claimed that in their efforts to achieve mature adulthood, children must overcome, outgrow, and sublimate their instinctual passions. Freud thus refutes Locke and confirms Rousseau: the mind is not a tabula rasa; the child's mind does approximate a "state of nature"; to some extent the demands of nature must be taken into account or permanent personality dysfunctions will result. But at the same time, Freud refutes Rousseau and confirms Locke: the earliest interactions between child and parents are decisive in determining the kind of adult the child will be; through reason, the passions of the mind may be controlled; civilization is quite impossible without repression and sublimation.

In a similar way, although from a framework of philosophy,

Dewey argued that the psychic needs of the child must be addressed in terms of what the child is, not what the child will be. At home and in school adults must ask, What does the child need *now*? What problems must he or she solve *now*? Only in this way, Dewey believed, will the child become a constructive participant in the social life of the community. "If we identify ourselves with the real instincts and needs of childhood," he wrote, "and [require] only [their] fullest assertion and growth . . . discipline and culture of adult life shall all come in their due season."[13]

Freud and Dewey crystallized the basic paradigm of childhood that had been forming since the printing press: the child as schoolboy or schoolgirl whose self and individuality must be preserved by nurturing, whose capacity for self-control, deferred gratification, and logical thought must be extended, whose knowledge of life must be under the control of adults. Yet at the same time, the child is understood as having its own rules for development, and a charm, curiosity, and exuberance that must not be strangled—indeed, is strangled— at the risk of losing mature adulthood.

All of the psychological research on childhood that has been done in this century—for example, by Jean Piaget, Harry Stack Sullivan, Karen Horney, Jerome Bruner, or Lawrence Kohlberg—has been mere commentary on the basic childhood paradigm. No one has disputed that children are different from adults. No one has disputed that children must *achieve* adulthood. No one has disputed that the responsibility for the growth of children lies with adults. In fact, no one has disputed that there is a sense in which adults are at their best, their most civilized, when tending to the nurture of children. For we must remember that the modern paradigm of childhood is also the modern paradigm of adulthood. In saying what we wish a child to become, we are saying what we are. One might go so far as to claim that to the extent that there has been any growth in empathy and sensibility—in simple humaneness— in Western civilization, it has followed the path of the growth of childhood. Four hundred years of our history refutes W. C. Fields's remark that he who hates children can't be all bad. Of course, one mustn't be unfair to a great comedian. The remark was intended as a joke, deriving its point from a malevolent irony. One wonders how Fields would make the joke today as childhood slips from our grasp.

PART 2

The Disappearance of Childhood

Chapter 5

The Beginning
of the End

The period between 1850 and 1950 represents the high-watermark of childhood. In America, to which we must now give our exclusive attention, successful attempts were made during these years to get all children into school and out of factories, into their own clothing, their own furniture, their own literature, their own games, their own social world. In a hundred laws children were classified as qualitatively different from adults; in a hundred customs, assigned a preferred status and offered protection from the vagaries of adult life.

This is the period during which the stereotype of the modern family was cast, and, if we accept Lloyd deMause's chronology, it is the period in which parents developed the psychic mechanisms that allow for a full measure of empathy, tenderness, and responsibility toward their children. This is not to say that childhood became idyllic. Like all stages of life, it was, and is, filled with pain and confusion. But by the turn of the century childhood had come to be regarded as every person's birthright, an ideal that transcended social and economic class. Inevitably, childhood came to be defined as a biological category, not a product of culture. Thus, it is a fascinating irony that during this same period, the symbolic environment that gave life to childhood began to be disassembled, slowly and inconspicuously.

If one were to designate a single person as the parent of the emerging childless age, it would have to be Professor Samuel Finley Breese Morse of New York University. For it was Morse who was mainly responsible for sending the first public electric message ever transmitted on this planet. Like Gutenberg, he had little idea of what his invention would lead to, although to his credit he explicitly acknowledged his ignorance in his famous electrically coded message, "What hath God wrought?"[1]

As a matter of historical interest, it should be noted that Morse's fascination with the communicative possibilities of electricity was aroused during a voyage in 1832 aboard the ship *Sully*. It was there that he first learned that electricity could be sent instantly over any known length of wire, and legend has it that as Morse disembarked from the ship he told the captain, "Should you hear of the telegraph one of these days, as the wonder of the world, remember the discovery was made on the good ship *Sully*."

While Morse was aboard the *Sully,* Charles Darwin was aboard H.M.S. *Beagle* making the observations that led to *The Origin of Species*. Conventional wisdom has it that Darwin's voyage, which began in December 1831, was a world-shattering event in that its result was to dislodge theological fancy and replace it with scientific hypotheses. Without meaning to dispute that wisdom, I should like to suggest that Morse's voyage had far more serious consequences for world culture than Darwin's. Darwin put forward ideas that have largely influenced scholars and theologians. It may be doubted that his theory has had much effect on the practical affairs of people or that it has much altered their institutions and habits of mind. As I write, millions of Americans are engaged in a struggle to defame the assumptions embodied in Darwinian thought. That their struggle is vain and pathetic is not to the point, which is, simply, that one can live without believing in evolution. But everyone must confront the conditions of electric communication. No matter where or how one lives, or by what creed, it is Morse, not Darwin, who dictates how one's affairs must be managed and how one's consciousness must be directed. This fact is a clear tribute not to Morse himself but to what Christine Nystrom has called the "invisible metaphysics" of technology. For there is this difference between Darwin and Morse: Darwin offered us ideas embodied in language. His ideas are explicit, arguable, and refutable. Indeed, they have been publicly debated since the 1860s in lecture halls, classrooms, and even courtrooms. But Morse offered us ideas embodied in a technology, which is to say, they were hidden from view and therefore never argued. Morse's ideas were, in a sense, irrefutable, because no one knew that electric communication implied any ideas. As is usually the case with communication technology, people assumed that the telegraph was a neutral conveyance, that it was partial to no world-view of its own. The only questions that were asked of Morse concerned whether or not the machine would work, how far its range, how expensive its development.

In saying no one knew about the ideas implicit in the telegraph, I am not quite accurate. Thoreau knew. Or so one may surmise. It is alleged that upon being told that through the telegraph a man in Maine could instantly send a message to a man in Texas, Thoreau asked, "But what do they have to say to each other?" In asking this question, to which no serious interest was paid, Thoreau was directing attention to the psychological and social meaning of the telegraph, and in particular to its capacity to change the character of information—from the personal and regional to the impersonal and global. A hundred and twenty years later Marshall McLuhan tried to address the issue Thoreau raised. He wrote:

> When man lives in an electric environment, his nature is transformed and his private identity is merged with

the corporate whole. He becomes "Mass Man." Mass
Man is a phenomenon of electric speed, not of physical
quantity. Mass Man was first noticed as a phenomenon
in the age of radio, but he had come into existence,
unnoticed, with the electric telegraph.[2]

In my opinion, McLuhan, whose metier was hyperbole, is
far from exaggerating the case here. The electric telegraph
was the first communication medium to allow the speed of
a message to exceed the speed of the human body. It broke
the historic connection between transportation and communication. Prior to the telegraph, all messages, including those
expressed in writing, could move only as fast as a human
being could carry one. The telegraph eliminated in one stroke
both time and space as dimensions of human communication,
and therefore disembodied information to an extent that far
surpassed both the written and printed word. For electric
speed was not an extension of human senses but a denial of
them. It took us into a world of simultaneity and instancy
that went beyond human experience. In doing so, it eliminated
personal style, indeed, human personality itself, as an aspect
of communication. From their beginnings, telegraphic messages were conveyed in a ritual language, a no-man's dialect
that left little room for the expression of individuality. I am
not referring here to the use of the telegraph as a kind of
instant letter, carrying greetings to those celebrating their
birthdays and anniversaries, although even in this the telegraph
employed largely denuded language. Rather, I refer to the
dominant use of the telegraph as a distributor of news. The
telegraph created the "news industry" by transforming information from a personal possession to a commodity of worldwide value. In the 1840s a national telegraphic news service
was developed by William Swain and Amos Kendall, and in
1848, the Associated Press was founded. As the country
became wired for electric speed, information, inevitably, became more important than its source. The metaphor to keep

in view here is the ancient tradition of executing the messenger who bears bad news—that is, the tradition of holding the speaker responsible for what he speaks—the ultimate compliment to personal identity. But with the electric telegraph, news became reified, spoken of as an "it" or a "they," as in "It says in the news . . ." or "They say that . . ." After the telegraph, no one was *responsible* for the news. Like the newspaper, the telegraph addressed the world, not individuals. But unlike the newspaper, its information had no identifiable source. To use Edward Epstein's phrase, the news came from nowhere. In fact, in one of Morse's early demonstrations he sent the message "Attention Universe." It was as if the telegraph itself were addressing the cosmos. Perhaps, after all, Morse *did* know.

In any case, the answer to Thoreau's question is, finally, that it does not matter what a man in Maine has to say to a man in Texas. Through the telegraph, men do not "say" anything in the sense Thoreau used the word. What the telegraph did was to create a world of anonymous, decontextualized information in which the differences between Maine and Texas became increasingly irrelevant. The telegraph also moved history into the background and amplified the instant and simultaneous present. But most important, *the telegraph began the process of making information uncontrollable*. As the telegraph gave us news from nowhere, it also gave it in unprecedented volume, for quantity of information is a function of the speed with which it can be generated and moved. News from nowhere means news from everywhere, about everything, and in no particular order. The telegraph created an audience and a market not only for news but for fragmented, discontinuous, and essentially irrelevant news, which to this day is the main commodity of the news industry. Prior to the telegraph, because of the technical difficulty of communicating information through space, news tended to be selective and pertinent to the lives of people, which is why Thoreau posed his question. After the telegraph, news became unselective and unusable, at least by the measure of a man like Thoreau. Indeed, it is stretching the point only a little to say that the telegraph helped to create a new definition of intelligence, for as the world became flooded with information, the question of how much one knew assumed more importance than the question of what uses one made of what one did know.

NB

All of this had the greatest possible significance for childhood. Childhood, as I have tried to show, was an outgrowth of an environment in which a particular form of information, exclusively controlled by adults, was made available in stages to children in what was judged to be psychologically assimilable ways. The maintenance of childhood depended on the principles of managed information and sequential learning. But the telegraph began the process of wresting control of information from the home and school. It altered the kind of information children could have access to, its quality and quantity, its sequence, and the circumstances in which it would be experienced.

Of course, had the possibilities of electric communication been exhausted by the telegraph, it is possible that the social and intellectual structure of the literate world would have remained largely intact, and that childhood in particular would not have been much affected. But the telegraph was only a foreshadowing of what was to follow. Between 1850 and 1950 the communication structure of America was dissolved, then reconstituted, by an uninterrupted flow of invention—the rotary press, the camera, the telephone, the phonograph, the movies, the radio, television. By including the rotary press and the camera, I mean to suggest that electric media were not the only factors leading to a new symbolic world. Paralleling the development of electric communication, there unfolded what Daniel Boorstin has called the "graphic revolution," the emergence of a symbolic world of pictures, cartoons, posters and advertisements.[3] Taken together, the electronic and the graphic revolutions represented an uncoordinated but powerful assault on language and literacy, a recasting of the world of ideas into speed-of-light icons and images.

The significance of this development cannot be exaggerated. For while speed of transmission made the management of information impossible, the mass-produced image changed the form of information itself—from discursive to nondiscursive, from propositional to presentational, from rationalistic to emotive. Language is an abstraction about experience, whereas pictures are concrete representations of experience. A picture may, indeed, be worth a thousand words, but it is in no sense the *equivalent* of a thousand words, or a hundred, or two. Words and pictures are different universes of discourse, for a word is always and foremost an idea, a figment, so to speak, of imagination. There does not exist in nature any such thing as "cat" or "work" or "wine." Such words are concepts about the regularities we observe in nature. Pictures do not show concepts; they show things. It cannot be said often enough that, unlike sentences, a picture is irrefutable. It does not put forward a proposition, it implies no opposite or negation of itself, there are no rules of evidence or logic to which it must conform.[4]

NB cf. Birkerts on Reading

Thus, there is a sense in which pictures and other graphic images may be said to be "cognitively regressive" (to use Reginald Damerall's phrase), at least in contrast to the printed word. The printed word requires of a reader an aggressive response to its "truth content." One may not always be in a position to make that assessment but, in theory, the assessment can be made—if only one had enough knowledge or experience. But pictures require of the observer an aesthetic response. They call upon our emotions, not our reason. They ask us to feel, not to think. This is why Rudolf Arnheim in reflecting on the graphic revolution and anticipating its massive manifestation on television warned that it has the potential to put our minds to sleep. "We must not forget," he wrote,

that in the past the inability to transport immediate
experience and to convey it to others made the use of
language necessary and thus compelled the human mind
to develop concepts. For in order to describe things one
must draw the general from the specific; one must select,
compare, think. When communication can be achieved
by pointing with the finger, however, the mouth grows
silent, the writing hand stops, and the mind shrinks.[5]

This observation was made in 1935, before the full maturing
of the image-information environment. Forty-five years later,
Arnheim's prophecy was ruefully acknowledged as fact by
Robert Heilbroner in his claim that pictorial advertising has
been the single most destructive force in undermining the
assumptions of the literate world.[6] In saying this, he meant to
suggest, as has Roland Barthes, that the mass-produced image
has introduced a constant and pervasive element of irratio-
nalism into both politics and commerce.[7] With the photograph,
then movies, and finally television, a candidate's "image" has
become more important than his plans, a product's "image"
more important than its usefulness. In making these judgments,
Arnheim, Heilbroner, and Barthes indicate by implication how
the graphic revolution has contributed to a radical change in
the status of childhood. For they are talking about the
emergence of a symbolic world that cannot support the social
and intellectual hierarchies that make childhood possible.

Before explicating the details of the transformation now
taking place, I must mention, once again, the irony of the
situation: During the period between 1850 and 1950 enormous
effort was expended in getting America to become literate, in
elevating the values of the literate attitude. But at exactly the
same time, electric speed and mass-produced imagery were
working together to undermine that effort and attitude. By
1950 the competition between the two symbolic worlds finally
became visible and the irony manifest. Like many other social
artifacts, childhood became obsolete at the same time that it

was perceived as a permanent fixture. I choose 1950 because
by that year television had become firmly installed in American
homes, and it is in television that we have the coming together
of the electric and graphic revolutions. It is in television,
therefore, that we can see most clearly how and why the
historic basis for a dividing line between childhood and adulthood is being unmistakably eroded.

The period in which we live is, of course, the incunabula
of television. After the invention of the printing press it took
sixty years for printers to arrive at the idea of numbering the
pages of books. Who knows what the future holds for television? There may be novel and profound uses for it that will be
thought of by people not yet born. But if we consider broad-
cast commercial television as we presently know it, we can
see in it, quite clearly, a paradigm of an emerging social structure that must "disappear" childhood. There are several reasons
for this, one of which I shall deal with here, the others in the
following two chapters.

The first concerns the idea of accessibility of information,
which, in turn, is related to the form in which information is
encoded. The changeover from a pictographic writing system
to the alphabet 3,500 years ago is a good example of the
point I wish to make here.[8] Prior to the invention of the
alphabet, "readers" were required to learn an enormous number of signs in order to interpret a written message. The task
was so arduous that only a few could achieve it, and those who
did were required to devote their lives to it. But it was worth
it. As a result of their exclusive skills they accumulated vast
political and religious power, as is always the case when a
group has knowledge of secrets to which the general population is denied access. Pictographic writing, in other words,
generated a particular social, political, and religious structure.
With the coming of the alphabet, as Isaac Taylor has observed
in *The History of the Alphabet,* this structure was overthrown.[9]
The priests and scribes had their "knowledge monopoly"
shattered by a relatively simple and ingenious writing system

that opened the secrets of the written word to large numbers of people.

In a similar way, the book culture of the sixteenth through twentieth centuries created another knowledge monopoly—this time, separating children and adults. A fully literate adult had access to all of the sacred and profane information in books, to the many forms of literature, to all of the recorded secrets of human experience. Children, for the most part, did not. Which is why they were children. And why they were required to go to school.

To be sure, the printed English alphabet is much easier to learn than were Sumerian pictographs, which is why most children could achieve adulthood. But phonetic literacy is not altogether simple to learn, and for two reasons. In the first place, because mature reading is an act of immediate recognition, that is, an unconscious reflex, the habit of reading must be formed in that period when one is still in the process of acquiring oral language. People who try to learn how to read after their oral language is completed rarely, if ever, become fluent readers.[10] Thus, reading instruction must begin at an early age, when children are not biologically suited to the rigors of immobility. This is one reason why many children have difficulty becoming easy readers. Another, and far more important, reason is that learning to read is not simply a matter of learning to "crack the code." When one learns to read, one learns a peculiar way of behaving of which physical immobility is only one feature. Self-restraint is a challenge not only to the body but to the mind as well. Sentences, paragraphs, and pages unfold slowly, in sequence, and according to a logic that is far from intuitive. In reading, one must wait to get the answer, wait to reach the conclusion. And while waiting, one is obliged to evaluate the validity of the sentences, or at least know when and under what conditions to suspend critical judgment.

To learn to read is to learn to abide by the rules of a complex logical and rhetorical tradition that requires one to take the measure of sentences in a cautious and rigorous way, and, of course, to modify meanings continuously as new elements unfold in sequence. The literate person must learn to be reflective and analytical, patient and assertive, always poised, after due consideration, to say no to a text. This mode of behavior is difficult for the young to learn. Indeed, it must be learned in stages, which is why the young reader is expected, at first, only to paraphrase, not criticize. And why an eight-year-old is not expected to read *The New York Times,* let alone Plato's *Republic.* It is also why, since the sixteenth century, adults have had a strong impulse to censor the reading matter of children, the assumption being that children do not yet have sufficient command of the "literate attitude" to suspend belief. (Children apparently have far less difficulty in suspending *dis*belief.) With some exceptions adult reading behavior is rarely achieved before the age of fourteen or fifteen (and, of course, in some cases not at all). Here it must be borne in mind that the school curriculum itself has always been the most stringent and persistent expression of adult-imposed censorship. The books that are read in the fourth grade or seventh grade or ninth are chosen not only because their vocabulary and syntax are judged to be suitable for a given age but also because their content is considered to contain fourth-, seventh-, or ninth-grade information, ideas, and experience. The assumption is that a fourth grader does not yet know about seventh-grade experience, nor a seventh grader about ninth-grade experience. Such an assumption could be rationally made in a print-based culture, for up until the present day the printed word, for all of its seeming accessibility, has been sufficiently difficult to master, and the literate attitude sufficiently difficult to achieve, that both have effectively functioned as a barrier between the child and the adult, even between the young child and the adolescent.

But with television, the basis of this information hierarchy collapses. Television is first and foremost a visual medium, which Arnheim understood in 1935 but which devotees of

Sesame Street still have not grasped. Although language is heard on television, and sometimes assumes importance, it is the picture that dominates the viewer's consciousness and carries the critical meanings. To say it as simply as one can, *people watch television*. They do not read it. Nor do they much listen to it. They watch it. This is true of adults and children, intellectuals and laborers, fools and wise men. And what they watch are dynamic, constantly changing images, as many as 1,200 different ones every hour. One of the more naïve delusions about television is that there can be great variability in the conceptual level of programs. Such variability is, indeed, possible when television is used to replicate the lecture hall, as in the case of *Sunrise Semester,* where all that is seen on the screen is a "talking head" from which there issues forth a stream of sentences. Because it is in the nature of sentences that they may be true or false, complex or simple, intelligent or stupid, the conceptual level of *Sunrise Semester* may vary greatly. But television is rarely used in this way, for the same reason that a 747 jet aircraft is not used to carry mail from New York City to Newark: it is badly suited to the task. In particular, television is *not* a lecture hall. It is an image show, a pictographic medium, not a linguistic one. That is why even such "highbrow" programs as *The Ascent of Man* and *Cosmos,* to the extent that they strive to be good television programs, must make their focal point of attention the ever-changing visual image. (That is also why, not incidentally, *Cosmos* turns out to be mostly about the personality of Carl Sagan.) It is well to remember that the average length of a shot on a network television program is somewhere between three and four seconds, the average length of a shot on a commercial, between two and three seconds. This means that watching television requires instantaneous pattern-recognition, not delayed analytic decoding. It requires perception, not conception.

Television offers a fairly primitive but irresistible alternative to the linear and sequential logic of the printed word and tends to make the rigors of a literate education irrelevant. There are no ABC's for pictures. In learning to interpret the meaning of images, we do not require lessons in grammar or spelling or logic or vocabulary. We require no analogue to the McGuffey Reader, no preparation, no prerequisite training. Watching television not only requires no skills but develops no skills. As Damerall points out, "No child or adult becomes better at watching television by doing more of it. What skills are required are so elemental that we have yet to hear of a television viewing disability."[11] Unlike books, which vary greatly in their lexical and syntactical complexity and which may be scaled according to the ability of the reader, the TV image is available to everyone, regardless of age. According to studies by Daniel Anderson and others, children begin to watch TV with systematic attention by the age of thirty-six months, at which time they have favorite programs, can sing commercials, and are asking for products they see advertised.[12] But the programs, commercials, and products are not just for three-year-olds. There is no reason for them to be. So far as symbolic form is concerned, *Laverne & Shirley* is as simple to grasp as *Sesame Street;* a McDonald's commercial as simple to grasp as a Xerox commercial. Which is why, in truth, there is no such thing on TV as children's programming. Everything is for everybody.

The essential point is that TV presents information in a form that is undifferentiated in its accessibility, and this means that television does not need to make distinctions between the categories "child" and "adult." Indeed, in case I am suspected of exaggerating the point, it is worth saying that approximately 3 million children (age two to eleven) are watching television every night of the year between 11:00 P.M. and 11:30 P.M.; 2.1 million are watching between 11:30 P.M. and midnight; 1.1 million between 12:30 A.M. and 1:00 A.M.; and just under 750,000 between 1:00 A.M. and 1:30 A.M.[13] This happens not only because the symbolic form of television poses no cognitive mysteries but also because a television set cannot be hidden in a drawer or placed on a high shelf, out of the reach of children: its physical form, no less than its symbolic form, does not lend itself to exclusivity.

We may conclude, then, that television erodes the dividing line between childhood and adulthood in three ways, all having to do with its undifferentiated accessibility: first, because it requires no instruction to grasp its form; second, because it does not make complex demands on either mind or behavior; and third, because it does not segregate its audience. With the assistance of other electric, nonprint media, television re-creates the conditions of communication that existed in the fourteenth and fifteenth centuries. Biologically we are all equipped to see and interpret images and to hear such language as may be necessary to provide a context for most of these images. The new media environment that is emerging provides everyone, simultaneously, with the same information. Given the conditions I have described, electric media find it impossible to withhold any secrets. Without secrets, of course, there can be no such thing as childhood.

Chapter 6

The Total Disclosure Medium

Vidal Sassoon is a famous hairdresser who, for a while, had his own television show—a mixture of beauty hints, diet information, celebrity adoration, and popular psychology. As he came to the end of one segment of one of his programs, the theme music came up and Sassoon just had time enough to say, "Don't go away. We'll be back with a marvelous new diet and, then, a quick look at incest."

Phil Donahue, as of this writing, has a television show that appears five times a week. He is a serious and responsible person who apparently believes that any subject can be—indeed, ought to be—"treated" on television. But even if he did not believe this, he would do so anyway: five shows a week, an hour a day, fifty-two weeks each year, leave little room for squeamishness, selectivity, or even old-fashioned embarrassment. After one has "treated" the defense budget, the energy crisis, the women's movement, and crime in the streets, one inevitably must turn, whether quickly or slowly, to incest, promiscuity, homosexuality, sadomasochism, terminal illness, and other secrets of adult life. One may even turn to a kind of psychic striptease: the Stanley Siegel show, for example, regularly featured a segment in which its high-strung host reclined on a couch while a psychiatrist "analyzed" his feelings about his parents, his sexuality, and his precarious sense of personal identity.

For the moment, we must set aside the question of television's trivialization of culture. (What, for example, would Sophocles make of anyone's attempt to take a "quick look" at incest? What would Freud make of psychoanalysis being used as a vaudeville act?) There is a prior question that must be addressed: Why is television forcing the entire culture to come out of the closet? Why has the subject matter of the psychiatrist's couch and the Confessional Box come so un-ashamedly into the public domain?

The answer, I think, is obvious, although, to be sure, there are those who obscure it by pressing on us naïve theories about the malevolence of television executives. The plain facts are that television operates virtually around the clock, that both its physical and symbolic form make it unnecessary—in fact, impossible—to segregate its audience, and that it re-quires a continuous supply of novel and interesting informa-tion to engage and hold that audience. Thus, television must make use of every existing taboo in the culture. Whether the taboo is revealed on a talk show, made into a theme for a soap opera or situation comedy, or exposed in a commercial is largely irrelevant. Television needs material. And it needs it in a way quite different from other media. Television is not only a pictorial medium, it is a present-centered and speed-of-light medium. The bias and therefore the business of television is to *move* information, not collect it. Television cannot dwell upon a subject or explore it deeply, an activity for which the static, lineal form of typography is well suited. There may, for example, be fifty books on the history of Argentina, five hundred on childhood, five thousand on the Civil War. If television has anything to do with these subjects, it will do it once, and then move on. This is why television has become the principal generator of what Daniel Boorstin calls the "pseudo-event," by which he means events that are staged for public consumption.[1] The Academy Awards, the Miss America Contest, the "roasts" of celebrities, the Annual Country Music Association Awards, the battles of the network stars, press conferences, and the like exist because of television's need for material, not reality's. Television does not record these events; it creates them. And it does so not because television executives lack imagination but because they have an abundance of it. They know that television creates an insatiable need in its audience for novelty and public disclosure and that the dynamic visual imagery of television is not for the specialist, the researcher, or, indeed, for anyone wishing to practice analytic activity. To use a metaphor favored by Dorothy Singer, Jerome Singer, and Diana Zuckerman, watching television is like attending a party populated by people whom you do not know.[2] Every few seconds you are introduced to a new person as you move through the room. The general effect is one of excitement, but in the end it is hard to remember the names of the guests or what they said or even why they were there. It is of no importance that you do, in any case. Tomorrow there will be another party. To this image must be added the fact that you will be induced to return by the promise not only of new guests to meet but of the possibility that each of them will disclose a secret of some considerable interest. In other words: Don't go away. Tomorrow we'll take a quick look at incest.

The party

As long as the present system of competitive, commercial broadcasting exists, this situation will persist. One suspects that if every network executive and program director were replaced tomorrow by, say, the faculty of the Harvard Divinity School, television programming would in the long run remain quite close to what it is.[3]

Like alphabetic writing and the printed book, television opens secrets, makes public what has previously been private.[4] But unlike writing and printing, television has no way to close things down. The great paradox of literacy was that as it made secrets accessible, it simultaneously created an ob-

stacle to their availability. One must *qualify* for the deeper
mysteries of the printed page by submitting oneself to the
rigors of a scholastic education. One must progress slowly,
sequentially, even painfully, as the capacity for self-restraint
and conceptual thinking is both enriched and expanded. I
vividly remember being told as a thirteen-year-old of the
existence of a book, Henry Miller's *Tropic of Cancer,* that,
I was assured, was required reading for all who wanted to
know sexual secrets. But the problems that needed to be
solved to have access to it were formidable. For one, it was
hard to find. For another, it cost money. For still another,
it had to be *read.* Much of it, therefore, was not understand-
able to me, and even the special passages to which my attention was drawn by a thoughtful previous reader who under-
lined them required acts of imagination that my experience
could not always generate.

Television, by contrast, is an open-admission technology to
which there are no physical, economic, cognitive, or imaginative restraints. The six-year-old and the sixty-year-old are
equally qualified to experience what television has to offer.
Television, in this sense, is the consummate egalitarian medium of communication, surpassing oral language itself. For
in speaking, we may always whisper so that the children will
not hear. Or we may use words they may not understand.
But television cannot whisper, and its pictures are both concrete and self-explanatory. The children see everything it
shows.

The most obvious and general effect of this situation is to
eliminate the exclusivity of worldly knowledge and, therefore,
to eliminate one of the principal differences between childhood and adulthood. This effect follows from a fundamental
principle of social structure: A group is largely defined by the
exclusivity of the information its members share. If everyone
knew what lawyers know, there would be no lawyers. If
students knew what their teachers know, there would be no
need to differentiate between them. Indeed, if fifth graders

knew what eighth graders know, there would be no point to having grades at all. G. B. Shaw once remarked that all professions are conspiracies against the laity. We might broaden this idea to say that any group is a "conspiracy" against those who are not in it by virtue of the fact that, for one reason or another, the "outs" do not have access to the information possessed by the "ins."

Of course, not every instance of role differentiation or group identity rests on access to information. Biology, for example, will determine who will be a male and who a female.[5] But in most instances social role is formed by the conditions of a particular information environment, and this is most certainly the case with the social category of childhood. Children are a group of people who do *not* know certain things that adults know. In the Middle Ages there were no children because there existed no means for adults to know exclusive information. In the Age of Gutenberg, such a means developed. In the Age of Television, it is dissolved.

This means more than that childhood "innocence" is lost, a phrase that tends to imply only a diminution of childhood's charm. With the electric media's rapid and egalitarian disclosure of the total content of the adult world, several profound consequences result. First, the idea of shame is diluted and demystified. So that the meaning I am giving to shame may be clearer, it is necessary to introduce a particularly relevant remark by G. K. Chesterton. "All healthy men," he observed, "ancient and modern, Eastern and Western, know that there is a certain fury in sex that we cannot afford to inflame and that a certain mystery and awe must ever surround it if we are to remain sane."

Although Chesterton is here talking about sexual impulses, his point has a wider meaning, and is, I think, a fair summary of Freud's and Elias's views on the civilizing process. Civilization cannot exist without the control of impulses, particularly the impulse toward aggression and immediate gratification. We are in constant danger of being possessed by barbarism, of being overrun by violence, promiscuity, instinct, egoism. Shame is the mechanism by which barbarism is held at bay, and much of its power comes, as Chesterton holds, from the mystery and awe that surround various acts. Included among these acts are thoughts and words, all of which are made mysterious and awesome by the fact that they are constantly hidden from public view. By hiding them, we make them mysterious; by making them mysterious, we regulate them. In some cases, adults may not even display their knowledge of such secrets to each other and must find relief in the psychiatrist's office or the Confessional Box. But in all cases it is necessary to control the extent to which children are aware of such matters. Certainly since the Middle Ages it has been commonly believed that the impulse toward violence, sexuality, and egoism is of particular danger to children, who, it is assumed, are not yet sufficiently governed by self-restraint. Therefore, the inculcation of feelings of shame has constituted a rich and delicate part of a child's formal and informal education. Children, in other words, are immersed in a world of secrets, surrounded by mystery and awe; a world that will be made intelligible to them by adults who will teach them, in stages, how shame is transformed into a set of moral directives. From the child's point of view, shame gives power and authority to adulthood. For adults know, whereas children do not, what words are shameful to use, what subjects are shameful to discuss, what acts are deemed necessary to privatize.

I should like to be especially clear on this point. I do not argue that the content of shame is created by the information structure of society. The roots of shame lie elsewhere, go very deep into the history and fears of a people, and are far beyond the scope and point of this book. I am, however, claiming that shame cannot exert any influence as a means of social control or role differentiation in a society that cannot keep secrets. If one lived in a society in which the law required people to be nude on public beaches, the shame in revealing certain parts of the body would quickly disappear. For clothing is a means of keeping a secret, and if we are deprived of the means of keeping a secret, we are deprived of the secret. Similarly, the shamefulness in incest, in violence, in homosexuality, in mental illness, disappears when the means of concealing them disappears, when their details become the content of public discourse, available for examination by everyone in a public arena. What was once shameful may become a "social problem" or a "political issue" or a "psychological phenomenon," but in the process it must lose its dark and fugitive character, as well as some of its moral force.

It is an oversimplification to argue, as do representatives of the Moral Majority, that such a situation necessarily and categorically signifies cultural degeneration. It is well to remember that different cultures form different taboos, and what is shameful in one often appears arbitrary to another. We also have reason to hope that the transformation of shameful behavior into "social problems" or "alternate life-styles" through public disclosure and consequent rationalization may, in some notable instances, represent a step toward a more humane sensitivity. Certainly it would be hard to defend the proposition that a healthy society demands that death, mental illness, and homosexuality remain dark and mysterious secrets. And it would be even less defensible to argue that adults ought not to approach these subjects in any but the most restricted circumstances. But that the opening of these subjects to all, in unbound circumstances, poses dangers and in particular makes the future of childhood problematic must be boldly faced. For if there are no dark and fugitive mysteries for adults to conceal from children, and then reveal to them as they think necessary, safe, and proper, then surely the dividing line between adults and children becomes dangerously thin. We have here, in other words, a Faustian bargain, and it is very sad to note that the only sizable group in the body politic that has so far grasped the point is that benighted movement known as the Moral Majority. For through them the question has been raised, What is the price of openness and candor?

There are many answers to that question, most of which we do not know. But it is clear that if we turn over to children a vast store of powerful adult material, childhood cannot survive. By definition adulthood means mysteries solved and secrets uncovered. If from the start the children know the mysteries and the secrets, how shall we tell them apart from anyone else?

manners

With the gradual decline of shame there is, of course, a corresponding diminution in the significance of manners. As shame is the psychological mechanism that overcomes impulse, manners are the exterior social expression of the same conquest. Everything from table manners to language manners to the manners of dress is intended to reveal the extent to which one has learned self-restraint; and it is at the same time a means of teaching self-restraint. As already noted, manners or civilité did not begin to emerge in elaborated forms among the mass of people until after the printing press, in large measure because literacy both demanded and promoted a high degree of self-control and delayed gratification. Manners, one might say, are a social analogue to literacy. Both require a submission of body to mind. Both require a fairly long developmental learning process. Both require intensive adult teaching. As literacy creates a hierarchical intellectual order, manners create a hierarchical social order. Children must earn adulthood by becoming both literate and well-mannered. But in an information environment in which literacy loses force as a metaphor of the structure of human development, the importance of manners must decline. The new media make distinctions among age groups appear invidious, and thus are hostile to the idea of a hierarchical social order.

NB

Consider, for example, the case of language manners. Within recent memory adults did not use certain words in the presence of children, who, in turn, were not expected to use them in the presence of adults. The question of whether or not children knew such words from other contexts was beside the point. Social propriety required that a public distinction be maintained between an adult's symbolic world and the child's. This custom, unknown in the Middle Ages, represented more than a pleasant social fiction. Linguistic restraint on the adult's part reflected a social ideal, i.e., a disposition to protect children from the harsh, sordid, or cynical attitudes so often implicit in brutal or obscene language. On the children's part, restraint reflected an understanding of their place in the social hierarchy, and in particular, the understanding that they were not yet entitled to the public expression of such attitudes. But, of course, with the blurring of role distinctions such linguistic deference loses its point. Today, this custom has so rapidly eroded that those who practice it are considered "quaint." It would appear that we are moving back toward a fourteenth-century situation where no words were considered unfit for a youthful ear.

In the face of all this, both the authority of adulthood and the curiosity of childhood lose ground. For like shame and manners they are rooted in the idea of secrets. Children are curious because they do not yet know what they suspect there is to know; adults have authority in great measure because they are the principal source of knowledge. The delicate balance between authority and curiosity is the subject of Margaret Mead's important book *Culture and Commitment: A Study of the Generation Gap*. In it she contends that we are moving into a world of new, rapidly changing, and freely accessible information in which adults can no longer serve as counselors and advisors to the young, leading to what she calls a crisis in faith. "I believe this crisis in faith," she writes, "can be attributed . . . to the fact that there are now no elders who know more than the young themselves about what the young are experiencing."[6]

If Dr. Mead is right—if the elders can no longer be relied on as a source of knowledge for the young—then she has misnamed her book, and, indeed, missed her own point. She has not made a study of the generation gap but a study of the disappearance of the generation gap. For in a world where the elders have no more authority than the young, there is no authority; the gap is closed, and everyone is of the same generation. And although I cannot agree with Dr. Mead that we have reached the point where "there are . . . no elders who know more than the young themselves about what the young are experiencing," I believe it is clear enough that because of their relentless revelations of all cultural secrets, the electric media pose a serious challenge both to the authority of adulthood and to the curiosity of children. Perhaps because Dr. Mead wrote her book during the emergence of the short-lived but much publicized counterculture movement, she assumed that youthful curiosity would not be impaired by the decline of adult authority. To a certain extent curiosity comes naturally to the young, but its development depends upon a growing awareness of the power of well-ordered questions to expose secrets. The world of the known and the not yet known is bridged by wonderment. But wonderment happens largely in a situation where the child's world is separate from the adult world, where children must seek entry, through their questions, into the adult world. As media merge the two worlds, as the tension created by secrets to be unraveled is diminished, the calculus of wonderment changes. Curiosity is replaced by cynicism or, even worse, arrogance. We are left with children who rely not on authoritative adults but on news from nowhere. We are left with children who are given answers to questions they never asked. We are left, in short, without children.

We must keep in mind here that it is not television alone that contributes to the opening of adult secrets. As I have already noted, the process whereby information became uncontrollable—whereby the home and school lost their commanding place as regulators of child development—began with the telegraph and is not a new problem. Every medium of communication that plugs into a wall socket has contributed its share in freeing children from the limited range of childhood sensibility. The movies, for example, played a distinctive role in revealing to children the language and strategies of romance; those readers over the age of forty can testify to the fact that they learned the secrets of kissing from films. In today's world one can learn far more than that from a movie. But movies are not free, and it is still possible to bar children from those that display too much carnal knowledge or violence or adult madness. Except, of course, when they are shown on television. For with television there are no restrictions, economic or otherwise, and the occasional warning to parents that the "following program contains adult material . . . etc." only serves to ensure that more, not fewer, children will watch. What is it that they will see? What precisely are the secrets that will be revealed to them?

There are, as already mentioned, all of those matters that fall within the province of sexuality. Indeed, in revealing the secrets of sex, television has come close to eliminating the concept of sexual aberration altogether. For example, it is now common enough to see twelve- and thirteen-year-old girls displayed on television commercials as erotic objects. Some adults may have forgotten when such an act was regarded as psychopathic, and they will have to take my word for it that it was. This is not to say that adult males did not until recently covet pubescent girls. They did, but the point is that their desire was kept a carefully guarded secret, especially from the young themselves. Television not only exposes the secret but shows it to be an invidious inhibition and a matter of no special consequence. As in the Middle Ages, playing with the privy parts of children may once again become only a ribald amusement. Or, if that takes the matter too far, perhaps we may say that the explicit, albeit symbolic, *use* of children as material for the satisfaction of adult sexual fantasies has already become entirely acceptable. Indeed, conditioned by such use of children on television, the New York State Court of Appeals ruled in 1981 that no distinction may be made between children and adults in addressing the question of a pornographic film. If a film is judged obscene, the court ruled, then a conviction can be sustained. But if it is not judged obscene, then any law that tries to distinguish between the status of children and adults is invidious.[7] One might say that such a ruling clears the way for continued exploitation of children. Or, from another point of view, that such a ruling merely reflects the realities of our new electric environment. For there are, in fact, very few expressions of human sexuality that television now regards as serious enough to keep private, that is to say, regards as inappropriate for use as a theme for a program or as the focal point of a commercial. From vaginal spray commercials to discussions of male strippers, from programs preoccupied with the display of buttocks and breasts to documentaries on spouse swapping, the secrets unfold one by one, in one form or another. In some cases, to be sure, a subject such as incest, lesbianism, or infidelity is treated with seriousness and even dignity, but this is quite beside the point.

So that readers will not think these observations are merely the outpourings of a prudish sensibility, I should like to make my point as clearly as I can: The problem being discussed here is the difference between public knowledge and private knowledge, and what the effects are of the elimination of private knowledge by full-disclosure media. It is one thing to say that homosexuality is a sin in God's eyes, which I believe to be a dangerous idea. It is altogether different to say that something is lost when it is placed before children's eyes. It is one thing to say that human sexuality is base and ugly, which, in my opinion, is another dangerous idea. It is altogether different to say that its public display deprives it of its mystery and awe and changes the character and meaning of both sexuality and child development.

I am well aware that the word *hypocrisy* is sometimes used to describe a situation where public knowledge and private knowledge are rigidly kept apart. But the better face of hypocrisy is, after all, a certain social idealism. In the case of childhood, for example, secrecy is practiced in order to maintain the conditions for healthy and ordered growth. Child-hood, as we ideally think of it, cannot exist without a certain measure of hypocrisy. Let us take violence, for example. There can be no denying that human beings spend an in-ordinate amount of time and energy in maiming and killing each other. Along with symbol making and toolmaking, kill-ing is among our most distinctive characteristics. I have esti-mated that in my lifetime approximately seventy-five million people have been killed by other people. And this does not include those killings that are done, as Russell Baker puts it, in the name of private enterprise, e.g., street killings, family killings, robbery killings, etc. Is it hypocrisy to keep this knowledge from children? Hypocrisy should be made of sterner stuff. We wish to keep this knowledge from children because for all of its reality, too much of it too soon is quite likely dangerous to the well-being of an unformed mind. Enlightened opinion on child development claims it is neces-sary for children to believe that adults have control over their impulses to violence and that they have a clear conception of right and wrong. Through these beliefs, as Bruno Bettelheim has said, children can develop the positive feelings about them-selves that give them the strength to nurture their rationality, which, in turn, will sustain them in adversity.[8] C. H. Wad-dington has hypothesized that "one component of human evolution and the capacity for choice is the ability of the human child to accept on authority from elders the criteria for right and wrong."[9] Without such assurances children find it difficult to be hopeful or courageous or disciplined. If it is hypocrisy to hide from children the "facts" of adult violence and moral ineptitude, it is nonetheless wise to do so. Surely, hypocrisy in the cause of strengthening child growth is no vice.

This is not to say that children must be protected from all knowledge of violence or moral degeneracy. As Bettelheim has demonstrated in *The Uses of Enchantment,* the impor-tance of fairy tales lies in their capacity to reveal the existence

of evil in a form that permits children to integrate it without
trauma. This is possible not only because the content of fairy
tales has grown organically over centuries and is under the
control of adults (who may, for example, modify the violence or the ending to suit the needs of a particular child)
but also because the psychological context in which the tales
are told is usually reassuring and is, therefore, therapeutic.
But the violence that is now revealed over television is not
mediated by a mother's voice, is not much modified to suit
the child, is not governed by any theory of child development. It is there because television requires material that
comes in inexhaustible variety. It is also there because television directs everything to everyone at the same time, which
is to say, television cannot keep secrets of any kind. This
results in the impossibility of protecting children from the
fullest and harshest disclosure of unrelenting violence.

And here we must keep in mind that the stylized murders,
rapes, and plunderings that are depicted on weekly fictional
programs are much less than half the problem. They are,
after all, clearly marked as fiction or pseudo–fairy tales, and
we may assume (although not safely) that some children do
not take them to be representations of real adult life. Far
more impressive are the daily examples of violence and moral
degeneracy that are the staple of TV news shows. These are
not mitigated by the presence of recognizable and attractive
actors and actresses. They are put forward as the stuff of
everyday life. These are real murders, real rapes, real plunderings. And the fact that they *are* the stuff of real life makes
them all the more powerful.

Researchers have been trying for years to determine the
effects on children of such knowledge, their principal question being, To what extent does violence, when depicted so
vividly and on such a scale, induce violence in children?
Although this question is not trivial, it diverts our attention
from such important questions as, To what extent does the
depiction of the world *as it is* undermine a child's belief in

adult rationality, in the possibility of an ordered world, in a hopeful future? To what extent does it undermine the child's confidence in his or her future capacity to control the impulse to violence?

The secret of adult violence is, in fact, only part of a larger secret revealed by television. From the child's point of view, what is mostly shown on television is the plain fact that the adult world is filled with ineptitude, strife, and worry. Television, as Josh Meyrowitz has phrased it, opens to view the backstage of adult life. Researchers have paid very little attention to the implications of our revealing to children, in one televised form or another, the causes of marital conflict, the need for life insurance, the infinite possibilities of misunderstanding, the persistent incompetence of political leaders, the myriad afflictions of the human body. This list, which could be extended for a page, provides two items of particular interest as examples of how television is unsparing in revealing the secrets of adult life. The first, about which Meyrowitz has written with great insight, concerns the incompetence or at least vulnerability of political leaders. In its quest for material, especially of a "human interest" variety, television has found an almost inexhaustible supply in the private lives of politicians. Never before have so many people known so much about the wives, children, mistresses, drinking habits, sexual preferences, slips of the tongue, even inarticulateness of their national leaders. Those who did know at least some of this were kept informed by newspapers and magazines, which is to say that until television, the dark or private side of political life was mostly the business of adults. Children are not newspaper readers and never have been. But they are television viewers and therefore are continually exposed to accounts of the frailties of those who in a different age would have been perceived as without blemish. The result of this is that children develop what may be called adult attitudes—from cynicism to indifference—toward political leaders and toward the political process itself.

Similarly, children are kept constantly informed of the weaknesses of the human body, a matter that adults have typically tried to conceal from them. Of course, children have always known that people get sick and that in one way or another they die. But adults have found it wise to keep most of the details from children until a time when the facts will not overwhelm them. Television opens the closet door. For my own edification I counted the number of illnesses or physical impairments that were displayed on three consecutive evenings of network television. From hemorrhoids to the heartbreak of psoriasis, from neuritis and neuralgia to headaches and backaches, from arthritis to heart disease, from cancer to false teeth, from skin blemish to bad eyesight, there were forty-three references to the shocks our flesh is heir to. As if this were not enough to make life appear an uncertain, if not terrifying, journey, during the same period there were two references to the hydrogen bomb, a discussion of the inability of nations to stop terrorism, and a summary of the Abscam trials.

I am sure I have given the impression to this point that all of the adult secrets made available to children through television concern that which is frightening, sordid, or confusing. But in fact television is not necessarily biased in this direction. If most of its disclosures are of that nature, it is because most of adult life is of that naure, filled with illness, violence, incompetence, and disorder. But not all of adult life. There is, for example, the existential pleasure of buying things. Television reveals to children at the earliest possible age the joys of consumerism, the satisfactions to be derived from buying almost anything—from floor wax to automobiles. Marshall McLuhan was once asked why the news on television is always bad news. He replied that it wasn't: the commercials are the good news. And indeed they are. It is a comfort to know that the drudgery of one's work can be relieved by a trip to Jamaica or Hawaii, that one's status may be enhanced by buying a Cordoba, that one's competence may be established by using a certain detergent, that one's sex appeal may be enlivened by a mouthwash. These are the promises of American culture, and they give a certain coherence to adult motivations. By age three our children have been introduced to these motivations, for television invites everyone to share in them. I do not claim that these are mature motivations, and in fact in the next chapter I will try to show how television undermines any reasonable concept of mature adulthood. The point here is simply that the "good news" on television is *adult* good news, about which children are entirely knowledgeable by age seven.

Neither do I claim that children in an earlier period were entirely ignorant of the material of the adult world, only that not since the Middle Ages have children known so much about adult life as now. Not even the ten-year-old girls working in the mines in England in the eighteenth century were as knowing as our own children. The children of the industrial revolution knew very little beyond the horror of their own lives. Through the miracle of symbols and electricity our own children know everything anyone else knows—the good with the bad. Nothing is mysterious, nothing awesome, nothing is held back from public view. Indeed, it is a common enough observation, particularly favored by television executives when under attack, that whatever else may be said about television's impact on the young, today's children are better informed than any previous group of youngsters. The metaphor usually employed is that television is a window to the world. This observation is entirely correct, but why it should be taken as a sign of progress is a mystery. What does it mean that our children are better informed than ever before? That they know what the elders know? It means that they have become adults, or, at least, adult-like. It means—to use a metaphor of my own—that in having access to the previously hidden fruit of adult information, they are expelled from the garden of childhood.

Chapter 7

The Adult-Child

There is a well-traveled TV commercial for Ivory soap in which we are shown two women identified as a mother and daughter. The viewers are then challenged to guess which is the mother, which the daughter, both of whom appear to be in their late twenties and more or less interchangeable. I take this commercial to be an uncommonly explicit piece of evidence supporting the view that the differences between adults and children are disappearing. Although many other commercials imply as much, this one speaks directly to the point that in our culture it is now considered desirable that a mother should not look older than her daughter. Or that a daughter should not look younger than her mother. Whether this means that childhood is disappearing or that adulthood is disappearing is merely a matter of how one wishes to state the problem: Without a clear concept of what it means to be an adult, there can be no clear concept of what it means to be a child. Thus, the idea on which this book is based—that our electric information environment is "disappearing" childhood—can also be expressed by saying that our electric information environment is disappearing adulthood.

As I have taken some pains to show, the modern idea of

adulthood is largely a product of the printing press. Almost all of the characteristics we associate with adulthood are those that are (and were) either generated or amplified by the requirements of a fully literate culture: the capacity for self-restraint, a tolerance for delayed gratification, a sophisticated ability to think conceptually and sequentially, a preoccupation with both historical continuity and the future, a high valuation of reason and hierarchical order. As electric media move literacy to the periphery of culture and take its place at the center, different attitudes and character traits come to be valued and a new diminished definition of adulthood begins to emerge. It is a definition that does not exclude children, and therefore what results is a new configuration of the stages of life. In the television age there are three. At one end, infancy; at the other, senility. In between there is what we might call the adult-child.

The adult-child may be defined as a grown-up whose intellectual and emotional capacities are unrealized and, in particular, not significantly different from those associated with children. Such grown-ups have always existed, but cultures vary in the degree to which they encourage or discourage this characterological pattern. In the Middle Ages the adult-child was a normal condition, in large measure because in the absence of literacy, schools, and civilité no special discipline or learning was required in order to be an adult. For somewhat similar reasons the adult-child is emerging as normal in our own culture. I shall reserve for the next chapter putting forward the evidence that this is, indeed, happening. The purpose of this chapter is to show how and why it is happening.

The short answer is implied in what I have been saying: As the symbolic arena in which human growth takes place changes in its form and content, and in particular, changes in the direction of requiring no distinction between child and adult sensibilities, inevitably the two stages of life merge into one.

That is the theory. The long answer is mere commentary. Nonetheless, that is what follows.

In considering the ways in which the modern adult-child is created, we have available several entry points but none more interesting than the meaning of political consciousness and judgment in a society in which television carries the major burden of communicating political information. Before television, as noted in the previous chapter, it was relatively easy to control the amount and kind of information about political leaders that was made available to the public. After television, it has become so difficult to do so that those aspiring to political office must employ "image managers" in an attempt to control what the public knows. One of the important reasons for this shift is, of course, the sheer quantity of information television provides. More important is the form of the information.

Our political leaders, like everyone else, not only give information in the form of linguistic statements but also "give off" information through nonverbal means. How they stand, smile, fix their gaze, perspire, show anger, etc., tell as much about them as anything they might say. Naturally, it is much more difficult to control what they "give off" than what they give, which is why Richard Nixon could not shake his image as a used-car salesman, and Gerald Ford his image as an oaf. Television is largely responsible for these enduring perceptions because it reveals with precision most of the information given off by the living images on the screen. It is, in fact, a mistake for us to continue to use the phrase "television audience," a metaphor taken over from radio. Even in those cases where the image remains relatively fixed, as during a presidential address, the image is still at the center of one's consciousness, demanding interpretation and in sharp competition with spoken language. Where the TV image is constantly changed, as is normally the case, the viewer is entirely occupied with, if not overwhelmed by, nonverbal information. Television, to put it simply (and, I fear, repetitiously), does not call one's attention to ideas, which are abstract, distant, complex, and sequential, but to personalities, which are concrete, vivid, and holistic.

What this means is that the symbolic form of political information has been radically changed. In the television age, political judgment is transformed from an intellectual assessment of propositions to an intuitive and emotional re- sponse to the totality of an image. In the television age, people do not so much agree or disagree with politicians as like or dislike them. Television redefines what is meant by "sound political judgment" by making it into an aesthetic rather than a logical matter. A barely literate ten-year-old can interpret or at least respond to the information "given off" by a candidate as easily and quickly as a well-informed fifty-year-old. In fact, quite possibly more keenly. In any case, language and logic have almost nothing to do with the matter.

This alteration in the meaning of political judgment did not begin with television. It began in earnest as a side effect of the graphic revolution of the nineteenth century. But television so rapidly advances its course that we are justified in saying that with TV we descend to a qualitatively different level of political consciousness. And what makes this descent so interesting is that it represents a clear case of a conflict between the biases of an old medium and those of a new one. When the United States Constitution was written, James Madison and his colleagues assumed that mature citizenship necessarily implied a fairly high level of literacy and its concomitant analytic skills. For this reason, the young, commonly defined as those under twenty-one, were excluded from the electoral process because it was further assumed that the achievement of sophisticated literacy required training over a long period of time. These assumptions were entirely fitting in the eighteenth century in a society organized around the printed word, where political discourse was conducted largely through books, newspapers, pamphlets, and an oratory very much influenced by print. As Tocqueville tells us, the politics of America was the politics of the printed page.

Whatever other assumptions guided the development of our political structure (for example, concerning property ownership and race), none was more deeply ingrained than that adults and children are intellectually different and that adults have resources for the making of political judgments that the young do not have. While it may go too far to say, as George Counts once remarked, that the electric media have repealed the Bill of Rights, it is obvious that the making of political judgments in the Age of Television does not call upon the complex skills of literacy, does not even require literacy. How many Americans of voting age have ever *read* anything Ronald Reagan has ever written? Or have read anything written by those who have provided him with his ideology? How many were able to follow the arguments advanced in the presidential debates? How many believed that Ronald Reagan advanced arguments that Jimmy Carter or John Anderson could not refute?

Merely to ask such questions is to know, at once, how irrelevant they are, to realize what a minimal role ideological premises, logical consistency and force, or adeptness with language play in the assessment of a television image. If we may say that the Age of Andrew Jackson took political life out of the hands of aristocrats and turned it over to the masses, then we may say, with equal justification, that the Age of Television has taken politics away from the adult mind altogether. As Jackson changed the social arena, television has changed the symbolic arena in which politics is expressed and understood. Although the press has a vested interest in claiming that this is not so, everyone else recognizes that it is, especially those who run for office and those who are hired to show them how.

If this conclusion seems to exaggerate the situation, then consider the matter of public information as it is conveyed through television. To make a judgment about the quality of political consciousness, we must include an analysis of the character of the information available to citizens. It is well established that most Americans receive most of their information about the world through television, much of it through the format known as a television news show. What manner of experience do they have? What sort of information do they receive? What perspectives and insights are made available? In what sense, if any, is the public made knowledgeable? To what extent is a TV news show designed for the adult mind?

To understand what manner of thing a TV news show is —that is, any of the late news shows as seen in New York, Chicago, or San Francisco—we must look carefully at its structure. For example, all such shows begin and end with music; there is also music at every break for a commercial. What is its purpose? The same as in a theater or film: to excite the emotions of the audience, to create tension, to build expectations. But there is an important functional difference between, say, film music and TV news music in that in a film the music is varied according to the particular emotion the content calls for. There is frightening music, happy music, romantic music, and the like. On TV news shows, the same music is played whether the lead story is the invasion of Afghanistan or the adoption of a municipal budget or a Super Bowl victory. By using the same music each night, in the same spots, as an accompaniment to a *different* set of events, TV news shows contribute toward the development of their leitmotiv: that there are no important differences between one day and another, that the same emotions that were called for yesterday are called for today, and that in any case, the events of the day are meaningless.

This theme is developed through diverse means, including beauty, tempo, and discontinuity. Of beauty not much needs to be said beyond observing that TV newsreaders are almost all young and attractive—perhaps the handsomest class of people in America. Television, naturally enough, is biased toward compelling visual imagery, and in almost all cases the charms of a human face take precedence over the capabilities of a human voice. It is not essential that a TV newsreader grasp the meaning of what is being reported; many of them cannot even produce an appropriate facial display to go along with the words they are speaking. And some have even given up trying. What is essential is that the viewers like looking at their faces. To put it bluntly, as far as TV is concerned, in the United States there is not one sixty-year-old woman capable of being a newsreader. Viewers, it would appear, are not captivated by their faces. It is the teller, not what is told, that matters here.

It is also believed that audiences are captivated by variety and repelled by complexity, which is why, during a typical thirty-minute show, there will be between fifteen and twenty "stories." Discounting time for commercials, promos for stories to come, and newsreaders' banter, this works out to an average of sixty seconds a story. On a WCBS show chosen at random, it went like this one night: 264 seconds for a story about bribery of public officials; 37 seconds for a related story about Senator Larry Pressler; 40 seconds about Iran; 22 seconds about Aeroflot; 28 seconds about a massacre in Afghanistan; 25 seconds about Muhammad Ali; 53 seconds about a New Mexico prison rebellion; 160 seconds about protests against the film *Cruising;* 18 seconds about the owners of Studio 54; 18 seconds about Suzanne Somers; 16 seconds about the Rockettes; 174 seconds for an "in-depth" study of depression (Part I); 22 seconds about Lake Placid; 166 seconds for the St. John's–Louisville basketball game; 120 seconds for the weather; 100 seconds for a film review.

This way of defining the "news" achieves two interesting effects. First, it makes it difficult to think about an event, and second, it makes it difficult to feel about an event. By thinking, I mean having the time and motivation to ask oneself: What is the meaning of such an event? What is its history?

What are the reasons for it? How does it fit into what I know
about the world? By feeling, I mean the normal human responses to murder, rape, fire, bribery, and general mayhem.
During a survey I conducted some time ago, I was able to
identify only one story to which viewers responded with a
recollectable feeling of disgust or horror: the burning to death
of a "demon-possessed" baby by its mother. I believe there
is some significance in the fact that news shows will frequently
include thirty to forty-five seconds of "feeling" responses by
"the man and woman in the street," as if to remind the viewers
that they are *supposed* to feel something about a particular
story. I take this to be an expression of guilt on the part of
producers who know full well that their shows leave little
room for such reaction. On the WCBS show referred to, no
reactions were asked for about the massacre in Afghanistan
or the New Mexico prison riot. However, thirty-five seconds
were given over to "on the street" reactions to bribery charges
against Senator Harrison Williams of New Jersey. The people
allowed to comment said they felt terrible.

The point is, of course, that all events on TV come completely devoid of historical continuity or any other context,
and in such fragmented and rapid succession that they wash
over our minds in an undifferentiated stream. This is television as narcosis, dulling to both sense and sensibility. To
be sure, the music, the promos ("Coming up next, a riot in a
New Mexico prison . . ."), and the newsreaders' interactions
("What's happening in New Jersey, Jane?") create an air of
excitement, of tension to be resolved. But it is entirely ersatz,
for what is presented is so compressed and hurried—another
story fidgeting offstage, half mad with anxiety to do its thirty-
seven seconds—that one can scarcely retain in one's mind
the connection between the promise of excitement and its
resolution; that is to say, the excitement of a TV news show
is largely a function of tempo, not substance. It is excitement
about the movement of information, not its meaning.

But if it is difficult to think and feel about the news, this

must not be taken to mean that the viewer is not expected to
have a feeling, or at least an attitude, about the world. That
attitude, as I have said, is that all events, having no precedent
causes or subsequent consequences, are without value and
therefore meaningless. It must be kept in mind here that TV
news shows are terrifyingly surrealistic, discontinuous to the
point where almost nothing has anything to do with anything
else. What, for example, is the connection between Aeroflot
and Suzanne Somers? Between Studio 54 and Iran? Between
Cruising and a massacre in Afghanistan? Bribed officials and
the Rockettes? Will any of these stories be followed up? Were
they there yesterday? Why is Iran worth 40 seconds and the
St. John's game 166? How is it determined that Suzanne
Somers should get less time than Muhammad Ali? And what
in the end is the relationship of the commercials to the other
stories? There were, on the WCBS show, twenty-one commercials, occupying close to ten minutes. Three commercials preceded the bribery story, four commercials preceded the New
Mexico prison riot, three preceded the special report (Part I)
on depression. As you can well imagine, the commercials
were cheerful, filled with the promise of satisfaction, security,
and, in two cases, erotic pleasure.

Given such juxtapositions, what is a person to make of the
world? How is one to measure the importance of events?
What principles of human conduct are displayed, and according to what scheme of moral order are they valued? To any
such questions the TV news show has this invariable reply:
There is no sense of proportion to be discerned in the world.
Events are entirely idiosyncratic; history is irrelevant; there
is no rational basis for valuing one thing over another. The
news, in a phrase, is not an adult world-view.

Indeed, one cannot even find in this world-view a sense of
contradiction. Otherwise, we would not be shown four commercials celebrating the affluence of America, followed by
the despair and degradation of prisoners in a New Mexico

jail. One would have expected the newsreader at least to wink,
but he took no notice of what he was saying.

What all of this adds up to is that a television news show
is precisely what its name implies. A show is an entertainment, a world of artifice and fantasy carefully staged to produce a particular series of effects so that the audience is left
laughing or crying or stupefied. This is the business of a news
show, and it is puffery to claim, as producers do when they
accept their Emmy awards, that the purpose of such shows is
to make the public knowledgeable. The effect, of course, is
to trivialize the idea of Political Man, to erode the difference
between adult-like and childlike understanding.

This process is extended to areas other than the political.
For example, we may consider the decline of—indeed, the
merging of—Commercial Man and Religious Man. One of
the clear markers of an adult sensibility is the capacity to
distinguish between the commercial arena and the spiritual
one. And in most cultures the distinction is clear enough to
grasp. But in the Age of Television that distinction has become hopelessly muddled, in large measure because of the
omnipresent form of communication known as the television
commercial. Just as the news show alters the meaning of
political judgment, the TV commercial alters the meaning of
both consumership and religiosity.

So much has been written about commercials and their de-
grading suppositions and effects that it is difficult to find anything more to say. But certain things have not yet been given
sufficient attention insofar as they have a bearing on the
diminution of adulthood. For example, it must be stressed
that there is nothing in the form of TV commercials that requires that a distinction be made between adults and children.
TV commercials do not use propositions to persuade; they use
visual images, as for every other purpose. Such language as
is employed is highly emotive and only rarely risks verifiable
assertions. Therefore, commercials are not susceptible to

logical analysis, are not refutable, and, of course, do not require sophisticated adult judgment to assess. Ever since the graphic revolution, Commercial Man has been taken to be essentially irrational, not to be approached with argument or reasoned discourse. But on television this supposition is carried to such extremes that we may charge the television commercial with having rejected capitalist ideology altogether. That is to say, the television commercial has abandoned one of the key assumptions of mercantilism, which is that both buyer and seller are capable of making a trade based on a rational consideration of self-interest. This assumption is so deeply ingrained in capitalism that our laws severely restrict the commercial transactions children are allowed to make. In capitalist ideology, itself heavily influenced by the rise of literacy, it is held that children do not have the analytical skills to evaluate the buyer's product, that children are not yet fully capable of rational transactions. But the TV commercial does not present products in a form that calls upon analytic skills or what we customarily think of as rational and mature judgment. It is not facts that are offered to the consumer but idols, to which both adults and children can attach themselves with equal devotion and without the burden of logic or verification. It is, therefore, misleading even to call this form of communication "commercials," since they disdain the rhetoric of business and do their work largely with the symbols and rhetoric of religion. Indeed, I believe it is entirely fair to conclude that television commercials are a form of religious literature.

I do not claim that every television commercial has religious content. Just as in church the pastor will sometimes call the congregation's attention to nonecclesiastical matters, so there are TV commercials that are entirely secular in nature. Someone has something to sell; you are told what it is, where it can be obtained, and what it costs. Though these may be shrill and offensive, no doctrine is advanced and no theology invoked.

But the majority of important TV commercials take the form of religious parables organized around a coherent theology. Like all religious parables they put forward a concept of sin, intimations of the way to redemption, and a vision of Heaven. They also suggest what are the roots of evil and what are the obligations of the holy.

Consider, for example, The Parable of the Ring Around the Collar. This is to TV scripture what The Parable of the Prodigal Son is to the Bible, which is to say it is an archetype containing most of the elements of form and content that recur in its own genre. To begin with, The Parable of the Ring Around the Collar is short, occupying only about thirty seconds of one's time and attention. There are three reasons for this, all obvious. First, it is expensive to preach on television. Second, the attention span of the congregation is not long and is easily susceptible to distraction. And third, a parable does not need to be long; tradition dictates that its narrative structure be tight, its symbols unambiguous, its explication terse.

The narrative structure of The Parable of the Ring Around the Collar is, indeed, comfortably traditional. The story has a beginning, a middle, and an end. For those unfamiliar with it, a brief description is in order.

A married couple is depicted in some relaxed setting—say, a restaurant—in which they are enjoying each other's company and generally having a wonderful time. A waitress approaches their table, notices that the man has a dirty ring around his collar, stares at it boldly, sneers with cold contempt, and announces to all within hearing the nature of his transgression. The man is humiliated and glares at his wife with scorn. She, in turn, assumes an expression of self-loathing mixed with a touch of self-pity. This is the parable's beginning: the emergence of a problem.

The parable continues by showing the wife at home using a detergent that never fails to eliminate dirt around the collars of men's shirts. She proudly shows her husband what she is doing, and he forgives her with an adoring smile. This is the parable's middle: the solution of the problem. Finally, we are shown the couple in a restaurant once again, but this time they are free of the waitress's probing eyes and bitter social chastisement. This is the parable's end: the moral, the explication, the exegesis. From this we shall draw the proper conclusion.

In TV-commercial parables the root cause of evil is Technological Innocence, a failure to know the particulars of the beneficent accomplishments of industrial progress. This is the primary source of unhappiness, humiliation, and discord in life. And, as forcefully depicted in The Parable of the Ring, the consequences of technological innocence may strike at any time, without warning, and with the full force of their disintegrating action.

The sudden striking power of technological innocence is a particularly important feature of TV-commercial theology, for it is a constant reminder of the congregation's vulnerability. One must never be complacent or, worse, self-congratulatory. To attempt to live without technological sophistication is at all times dangerous, since the evidence of one's naïveté is painfully visible to the vigilant. The vigilant may be a waitress, a friend, a neighbor, or even a spectral figure—a holy ghost, as it were—who materializes in your kitchen, from nowhere, to give witness to your sluggish ignorance.

It must be understood, of course, that technological innocence is to be interpreted broadly, referring not only to ignorance of detergents, drugs, sanitary napkins, cars, salves, and foodstuffs, but also to technical machinery such as savings banks and transportation systems. One may, for example, come upon one's neighbors while on vacation (in TV-commercial parables, this is always a sign of danger) and discover that they have invested their money in a certain bank of whose special interest-rates you have been unaware. This is, of course, a moral disaster, and both you and your vacation are doomed.

But, as demonstrated in The Ring Parable, there is a road
to redemption. The road, however, has two obstacles. The
first requires that you be open to advice or social criticism ②
from those who are more enlightened. In The Ring Parable
the waitress serves the function of counselor, although she is,
to be sure, exacting and very close to unforgiving. In some
parables the adviser is rather more sarcastic than severe. But
in most parables, as for example in all sanitary-napkin, mouthwash, shampoo, and aspirin commercials, the advisers are
amiable and sympathetic, perhaps all too aware of their own
vulnerability in other matters.

The Innocent are only required to accept instruction in the
spirit in which it is offered. The importance of this cannot be
stressed enough, for it instructs the congregation in two lessons simultaneously: not only must one be eager to accept
advice, but one must be just as eager to give it. Giving advice
is, so to speak, the principal obligation of the holy. In fact,
the ideal religious community may be depicted in images of
dozens of people, each in his or her turn giving and taking
advice on technological advances.

The second obstacle on the road to redemption involves
one's willingness to act on the advice that is given. As in traditional Christian theology, it is not sufficient to hear the gospel
or even preach it. One's understanding must be expressed in
good works—i.e., action. In The Ring Parable the once piti-
able wife acts almost immediately, and the parable concludes
by showing the congregation the effects of her action.

In The Parable of the Person with Rotten Breath, of which
there are several versions, we are shown a woman who, ignorant of the technological solution to her unattractiveness, is
enlightened by a supportive roommate. The woman takes the
advice without delay, with results we are shown in the last
five seconds: a honeymoon in Hawaii. In The Parable of the
Stupid Investor, we are shown a man who knows not how
to make his money make money. Upon enlightenment he acts
swiftly, and, at the parable's end, he is rewarded with a car,

or a trip to Hawaii, or something approximating peace of mind.

Because of the compactness of commercial parables, the ending—that is, the last five seconds—must serve a dual purpose. It is, of course, the moral of the story: If one will act in such a way, this will be the reward. But in being shown the result, we are also shown an image of Heaven. Occasionally, as in The Parable of the Lost Traveler's Cheques, we are given a glimpse of Hell: Technical Innocents lost and condemned to eternal wandering far from their native land. But mostly we are given images of a Heaven both accessible and delicious: that is, a Heaven that is here, now, on Earth, in America, and quite often in Hawaii.

But Hawaii is only a convenient recurring symbol. Heaven can, in fact, materialize and envelop you anywhere. In The Parable of the Man Who Runs Through Airports, Heaven is found at a car-rental counter to which the confounded runner is shepherded by an angelic messenger. The expression of ecstasy on the runner's face tells clearly that this moment is as close to a sense of transcendence as he can ever hope for.

"Ecstasy" is the key idea here, for commercial parables depict the varieties of ecstasy in as much detail as you will find in any body of religious literature. At the conclusion of The Parable of the Spotted Glassware, a husband and wife assume such ecstatic countenances as can only be described by the word *beatification*. Even in The Ring Parable, which at first glance would not seem to pose as serious a moral crisis as spotted glassware, we are shown ecstasy, pure and serene. And where ecstasy is, so is Heaven. Heaven, in brief, is any place where you have joined your soul with the Deity—the Deity, of course, being Technology.

Just when, as a religious people, we replaced our faith in traditional ideas of God with a belief in the ennobling force of Technology is not easy to say. While it should be stressed that TV commercials played no role in bringing about this transformation, it is clear that they reflect the change, document it, amplify it, and in doing so, contribute to the diminution of mature spiritual orientations. As a consequence, they blur the line between adulthood and childhood, for children have no difficulty in understanding the theology of the TV commercial. There is nothing in it that is demanding or complex or that would inspire a profound question about the nature of existence. The adult who adopts this theology is no different from the child.

It is probably worthwhile to reiterate here that the childlike conception of political, commercial, and spiritual consciousness that is encouraged by television is not the "fault" of politicians, commercial hucksters, and TV executives who provide TV's content. Such people simply use television as they find it, and their motives are no better or worse than those of the viewers. To be sure, they exploit TV's resources, but it is the character of the medium not the character of the medium's users that produces the adult-child. This is an essential point to grasp. Otherwise we run the risk of deluding ourselves into believing that adulthood can be preserved by "improving" television. But television cannot be much improved, at least in the matter of its symbolic form or the context in which it is experienced or its speed-of-light movement of information. In particular, television is not a book, and can neither express the ideational content that is possible in typography nor further the attitudes and social organization associated with typography.

Television, for example, does not have effective resources for communicating a sense of either the past or the future. It is a present-centered medium. Everything on television is experienced as happening "now," which is why viewers must be told *in language* that the videotape they are seeing was made days or months before. As a consequence, the present is amplified out of all proportion, and it is a reasonable conjecture that adults are being forced by television into accepting as normal the childish need for immediate gratification, as well as childish indifference to consequences.

The context in which television is usually experienced is another matter of some importance. Like other media, such as radio and records, television tends to be an isolating experience, requiring no conformity to rules of public behavior. It does not even require that you pay attention, and, as a consequence, does nothing to further an adult awareness of social cohesion.

But undoubtedly the most significant aspect of television's structure is that which I have been so laboriously asserting: It expresses most of its content in visual images, not language. And, as a consequence, it must of necessity forgo exposition and use a narrative mode. This is why television's capacity to amuse is nearly inexhaustible. Television is the first true theater of the masses, not only because of the vast number of people it reaches but also because almost everything on television takes the form of a story, not an argument or a sequence of ideas. Politics becomes a story; news, a story; commerce and religion, a story. Even science becomes a story. That is why, as noted earlier, television programs such as *Cosmos* and *The Ascent of Man* are as visually dynamic and theatrical as anything else on TV; which is to say that Carl Sagan and Jacob Bronowski are presented—must be presented—as personalities, entertainers, and storytellers, surrounded by interesting things to look at. The science of Cosmology does not play well on television, and so we must watch Carl Sagan ride a bicycle as he tries to speak of it. Similarly, there is no way to televise a theory of cultural change, which is what Bronowski's *The Ascent of Man* was supposed to be about. But not one viewer in a hundred was aware of that fact, since his theory, as well as his supporting statements, was buried beneath a torrent of short-duration images. Only if the images were removed so that the language could be heard (as was the case when the script was printed in book form) could Bronowski's ideas become apparent and his questionable theory evaluated.

It is common to hear critics complain that TV appeals to

the lowest common denominator. But in what sense can we say of TV's images (e.g., Sagan riding a bicycle) that there is a higher intellect to which they can aspire? The superb science writer and professor of physics Jeremy Bernstein has put forward an answer of sorts in his critique of *Cosmos*.[1] Bernstein proposes that when a science program is presented, the visual image be kept stable, the professor on screen be situated behind a desk, and he or she simply talk. Assuming that the talk included complex facts, ideas, and conjectures, such a program would stimulate an educated imagination, Bernstein supposes. But such a program is not television. It is *Sunrise Semester*. It is television used to replicate the lecture hall or classroom, and it is doubtful that even those who aspire to the higher learning would watch for very long. Such people go to lecture halls and classrooms for what Professor Bernstein hopes they will learn. They expect something rather different from television, and those who produce programs provide it. As I write, WCBS is beginning commercial television's version of a "science show," for which a large audience is anticipated. It is called *Walter Cronkite's Universe*. No doubt Professor Bernstein, being an adult and an educated one, believes that the universe can speak well enough for itself and requires no boost from or association with Mr. Cronkite. WCBS knows better. And what WCBS knows is that the Age of Exposition, which was ushered in by the printing press and which gave the mind of the adult a special character, is very nearly over. It has been replaced by the Age of Narration, or, if one wants to be both more precise and picturesque, the Age of Show Business.

I do not use the phrase the Age of Show Business as a metaphor. I mean it to be taken literally, although there are two senses in which this might be done. First, it is in the nature of television to transform every aspect of life into a show-business format. Not only do we get *Walter Cronkite's Universe* (which could easily accommodate Don Rickles doing six minutes of outer space jokes and Lola Falana singing the theme song of *Star Wars*), we also get *Rex Humbard and His Family,* on location, bringing a message from God. Reverend Humbard is only one of a coven of preachers who, in using television, have assisted the TV commercial in accomplishing the near infantilization of theology. Surrounded by singers, members of their family, and exceedingly handsome people both on the stage and in the audience, these evangelists offer a religion that is as simplistic and theatrical as any Las Vegas act. No dogma, terminology, logic, ritual, or tradition are called upon to burden the minds of the viewers, who are required only to respond to the charisma of the preacher.

As noted, the same requirement is all that is asked of the news watcher. As I write, WNBC has just announced the signing of Tom Brokaw to a multi-year multimillion-dollar contract. For what? To read the news. One is tempted to wonder if Mr. Brokaw might profitably take his act to Las Vegas: "Tom Brokaw's World, featuring Don Rickles on Sports and Lola Falana as the Weatherwoman." But this would be redundant since his act on TV will reach a larger audience. The most striking example of the "show business" model of the world is *Sesame Street,* the highly acclaimed educational show for children. Its creators have accepted without reservation the idea that learning is not only *not* obstructed by entertainment but, on the contrary, is indistinguishable from it. In defending this conception of education, Jack Blessington, director of Educational Relations for WCBS, has observed "that there is a gap between kids' personal and cognitive development that schools don't know how to address." He went on to explain: "We live in a highly sophisticated, electronically oriented society. Print slows everything down."[2] Just so. Print means a slowed-down mind. Electronics means the speeded-up mind. One of the consequences of this fact— apparently unnoticed by Mr. Blessington—is that television "Las Vegasizes" our culture. The gap he speaks of is the difference between the slowed-down processes of thought encouraged by exposition and the fast-tempo responses required by a visually entertaining show. It goes without saying that *Sesame Street* in particular would do very nicely at prime time with both adults and children, not because of its alleged educational function but because, quite simply, it is a first-class act.

A second meaning of the phrase the Age of Show Business is related to the first but requires its own explanation. I refer to the fact that the business of television is to show—to forgo abstraction, to make everything concrete. And it is in this sense, as much as any other, that we can understand why adulthood is being diminished. We may pinpoint the issue by recalling what Lewis Carroll's Alice says just before beginning her adventures. Having nothing to do on a lazy day, Alice peeks at a book her sister is reading. But the book contains no pictures or conversations, by which Alice means stories. "And what is the use of a book," Alice thinks, "without pictures or conversations?" Lewis Carroll is making the obvious point that the pictorial and narrative mode is of a lower order of complexity and maturity than the expository. Pictures and stories are the natural form in which children understand the world. Exposition is for grown-ups.

If I may use Alice's question as a spur, What is the effect on grown-ups of a culture dominated by pictures and stories? What is the effect of a medium that is entirely centered on the present, that has no capability of revealing the continuity of time? What is the effect of a medium that must abjure conceptual complexity and highlight personality? What is the effect of a medium that always asks for an immediate, emotional response?

If the medium is as pervasive as television is, then we may answer in this way: Just as phonetic literacy altered the predispositions of the mind in Athens in the fifth century B.C., just as the disappearance of social literacy in the fifth century A.D. helped to create the medieval mind, just as typography enhanced the complexity of thought—indeed, changed the content of the mind—in the sixteenth century, then so does television make it unnecessary for us to distinguish between the child and the adult. For it is in its nature to homogenize mentalities. The often missed irony in the remark that television programs are designed for a twelve-year-old mentality is that there can be no other mentality for which they may be designed. Television is a medium consisting of very little but "pictures and stories," and Alice would have found it quite suitable for her needs.

In saying all of this, and in spite of how it may seem, I am not "criticizing" television but merely describing its limitations and the effects of those limitations. A great deal hinges on what we understand to be the nature of this great culture-transforming medium. Speaking at the commencement ceremonies at Emerson College in 1981, Leonard H. Goldenson, chairman of the board of ABC, told the graduates that ". . . we can no longer rely on our mastery of traditional skills. As communicators, as performers, as creators—and as citizens— [the electric revolution] requires a new kind of literacy. It will be a visual literacy, an electronic literacy, and it will be as much of an advance over the literacy of the written word we know today as that was over the purely oral tradition of man's early history."[3] Putting aside Mr. Goldenson's demonstration, as suggested in one of his sentences above, that he has himself already lost some mastery of traditional skills, I believe the first part of his statement to be entirely correct, although not in the sense he meant to imply. Television and other electric media do not, as he rightly says, require mastery of traditional skills. That is exactly my point, for it means that such skills will be impotent to encourage the differentiation of intellect that is necessary to sustain a distinction between adulthood and childhood. As for his statement that "visual literacy" will be as much of an advance over the literacy of the written word as that was over the oral tradition, one can only wonder what sort of advances Mr. Goldenson has in mind. Although it would be naïve and inaccurate to claim that literacy has been an unmixed blessing, the written, and then the printed, word brought a new kind of social organization to civilization. It brought logic, science, education, civilité; indeed, the very technology over which Mr. Goldenson presides. Thus, we may say that the literate mind has sown the seeds of its own destruction through the creation of media that render irrelevant those "traditional skills" on which literacy rests. It is a puzzlement to me that this fact should be a source of optimism to anyone save the chairman of the board of a television network.

Chapter 8

The Disappearing Child

To this point, my efforts have been directed at describing how the symbolic arena in which a society conducts itself will either make childhood necessary or irrelevant. I have, in particular, tried to explain how our new and revolutionary media are causing the expulsion of childhood after its long sojourn in Western civilization. It remains for me to put forward some of the direct evidence that this expulsion is indeed well under way.

The evidence for the disappearance of childhood comes in several varieties and from different sources. There is, for example, the evidence displayed by the media themselves, for they not only promote the unseating of childhood through their form and context but reflect its decline in their content. There is evidence to be seen in the merging of the taste and style of children and adults, as well as in the changing perspectives of relevant social institutions such as the law, the schools, and sports. And there is evidence of the "hard" variety—figures about alcoholism, drug use, sexual activity, crime, etc., that imply a fading distinction between childhood and adulthood. However, before presenting or pointing to any of it, I am obliged to acknowledge that the conjecture advanced in this book as to *why* this is happening cannot be proved, no matter how much evidence is marshaled in its favor. This is so not only because conjectures or theories can never be proved, even in the physical sciences, but also because in any effort at social science the very idea of proof or refutation is so encrusted with ambiguities and complexities that one can never be sure if the evidence has left a conjecture standing or has laid it low or is just plain irrelevant.

To illustrate: It has been claimed that the onset of puberty in females has been falling by about four months per decade for the past one hundred and thirty years, so that, for example, in 1900 the average age at which menstruation first occurred was approximately fourteen years, whereas in 1979 the average age was twelve years.[1] I rather fancy this statistic because, if true, it suggests that the contraction of childhood began to occur even in physiological terms shortly after the invention of the telegraph; that is, there is an almost perfect coincidence of the falling age of puberty and the communications revolution. I should therefore love to offer this as evidence in favor of my argument, but I rather think there are better explanations available, particularly those having to do with changes in diet.

To take another example: It is a certainty that the American household is shrinking. Today, there are only 2.8 persons per household, as compared to 4.1 in 1930. Or to look at it from another direction, in 1950, 10.9 percent of American households had only one person in them. Today, the figure is 22 percent.[2] Americans are not only having fewer children but apparently are spending less time nurturing them at home. Is this an effect of our changing communication environment? I believe it is, but one would be foolish to deny the contribution of other factors such as the increased affluence of Americans, their incredible mobility, the women's liberation movement, etc. In other words, as in this example, not only may there be multiple causation but, as in the first example, there well may be other theories to explain the facts. After all, in trying to account for changes in social organization or, indeed, for any cultural tendencies, there are many points from which one may embark. Marxists and Freudians, for example, would have ready explanations as to why childhood is disappearing, assuming that they agreed the evidence shows it is. Sociobiologists, anthropologists and—who knows?—perhaps even Scientific Creationists will not find themselves dry on the issue either. I have chosen the explanation offered in this book because insofar as any single perspective can be said to be tenable, this one best explains the facts. Indeed, nothing seems more obvious to me than that childhood is a function of what a culture needs to communicate and the means it has to do so. Although economics, politics, ideology, religion, and other factors affect the course of childhood—make it more or less important—they cannot create it or expunge it. Only literacy by its presence or absence has that power. I shall not, however, reargue this idea here. I wish only to say that I believe the idea is plausible, that it has at least a modest recommendation from the facts of history, and that it is supportable by present trends. The purpose of this chapter is to show that childhood *is* disappearing. After considering the evidence, the reader, inevitably, will decide if my theory is useful.

I should like to start, then, by calling attention to the fact that children have virtually disappeared from the media, especially from television. (There is absolutely no sign of them on radio or records, but their disappearance from television is more revealing.) I do not mean, of course, that people who are young in years cannot be seen. I mean that when they are shown, they are depicted as miniature adults in the manner of thirteenth- and fourteenth-century paintings. We might call this condition the Gary Coleman Phenomenon, by which I mean that an attentive viewer of situation comedies, soap operas, or any other popular TV format will notice that the children on such shows do not differ significantly in their interests, language, dress, or sexuality from the adults on the same shows.

Having said this, I must concede that the popular arts have rarely depicted children in an authentic manner. We have only to think of some of the great child stars of films, such as Shirley Temple, Jackie Coogan, Jackie Cooper, Margaret O'Brien, and the harmless ruffians of the Our Gang comedies, to realize that cinema representations of the character and sensibility of the young have been far from realistic. But one could find in them, nonetheless, an ideal, a *conception* of childhood. These children dressed differently from adults, talked differently, saw problems from a different perspective, had a different status, were more vulnerable. Even in the early days of television, on such programs as *Leave It to Beaver* and *Father Knows Best,* one could find children who were, if not realistically portrayed, at least different from adults. But most of this is now gone, or at least rapidly going.

Perhaps the best way to grasp what has happened here is to imagine what *The Shirley Temple Show* would be like were it a television series today, assuming of course that Miss Temple were the same age now as she was when she made her memorable films. (She began her career at age four but made most of her successful films between the ages of six and ten.) Is it imaginable except as parody that Shirley Temple would sing—let us say, as a theme song—"On the Good Ship Lollipop"? If she would sing at all, her milieu would be rock music, that is, music as much associated with adult sensibility as with that of youth. (See Studio 54 and other adult discos.) On today's network television there simply is no such thing as a child's song. It is a dead species, which tells as much about what I am discussing here as anything I can think of. In any case, a ten-year-old Shirley Temple would probably require a boyfriend with whom she would be more than occasionally entangled in a simulated lover's quarrel. She would certainly have to abandon "little girl's" dresses and hairstyles for something approximating adult fashion. Her language would consist of a string of knowing wisecracks, including a liberal display of sexual innuendo. In short, *The Shirley Temple Show* would not—could not—be about a child, adorable or otherwise. Too many in the audience would find such a conception either fanciful or unrecognizable, especially the youthful audience.

Of course, the disappearance from television of our traditional model of childhood is to be observed most vividly in commercials. I have already spoken of the wide use of eleven- and twelve-year-old girls as erotic objects (the Brooke Shields Phenomenon), but it is necessary to mention one extraordinary commercial for Jordache jeans in which both schoolgirls and schoolboys—most of them prepubescent—are represented as being driven silly by their undisciplined libidos, which are further inflamed by the wearing of designer jeans. The commercial concludes by showing that their teacher wears the same jeans. What can this mean other than that no distinction need be made between children and adults in either their sexuality or the means by which it is stimulated?

But beyond this, and just as significant, is the fact that children, with or without hyperactive libidos, are commonly and unashamedly used as actors in commercial dramas. In one evening's viewing I counted nine different products for which a child served as a pitchman. These included sausages, real estate, toothpaste, insurance, a detergent, and a restaurant chain. American television viewers apparently do not think it either unusual or disagreeable that children should instruct them in the glories of corporate America, perhaps because as children are admitted to more and more aspects of adult life, it would seem arbitrary to exclude them from one of the most important: selling. In any case, we have here a new meaning to the prophecy that a child shall lead them.

The "adultification" of children on television is closely paralleled in films. Such movies as different as *Carrie, The Exorcist, Pretty Baby, Paper Moon, The Omen, The Blue Lagoon, Little Darlings, Endless Love,* and *A Little Romance* have in common a conception of the child who is in social orientation, language, and interests no different from adults. A particularly illuminating way in which to see the shift in child film imagery that has taken place in recent years is to compare the Little Rascals movies of the 1930s with the 1976 film *Bugsy Malone,* a satire in which children play the roles of adult characters from gangster movies. Most of the humor in the Little Rascals films derived its point from the sheer incongruity of children emulating adult behavior. Although *Bugsy Malone* uses children as a metaphor for adults, there is very little sense of incongruity in their role playing. After all, what is absurd about a twelve-year-old using "adult" language, dressing in adult clothes, showing an adult interest in sex, singing adult songs? The point is that the Little Rascals' films were clearly comedy. *Bugsy Malone* comes close to documentary.

Most of the widely discussed changes in children's literature have been in the same direction as those of the modern media. The work of Judy Blume has been emulated by many other writers who, like Ms. Blume, have grasped the idea that "adolescent literature" is best received when it simulates in theme and language adult literature, and, in particular, when its characters are presented as miniature adults. Of course, I do not wish to give the impression that there are currently no examples in children's literature (or, for that matter, in television or movies) of children who are emphatically different from adults. But I do mean to suggest that we are now undergoing a very rapid reorientation in our popular arts in regard to the image of children. One might put the matter, somewhat crudely, in this way: Our culture is not big enough for both Judy Blume and Walt Disney. One of them will have to go, and as the Disney empire's falling receipts show, it is the Disney conception of what a child is and needs that is disappearing.[3] We are in the process of exorcising a two-hundred-year-old image of the young as child and replacing it with the imagery of the young as adult.

Although this is exactly what Ms. Blume, our modern

filmmakers, and TV writers are doing, no moral or social demerit may be charged against them. Whatever else one may say in criticism of our popular arts, they cannot be accused of indifference to social reality. The shuffling black, the acquisitive Jew, even (to some extent) the obedient and passive wife, have disappeared from view, not because they are insufficiently interesting as material but because they are unacceptable to audiences. In a similar way, Shirley Temple is replaced by Brooke Shields because the audience requires a certain correspondence between the imagery of its popular arts and social reality as it is experienced. The question of the extent to which, say, television reflects social reality is a complex one, for there are times when it lags slightly behind, times when it anticipates changes, times when it is precisely on target. But it can never afford to be off the mark by too great a margin or it ceases to be a popular art. This is the sense in which we might say that television is our most democratic institution. Programs display what people understand and want or they are canceled. Most people no longer understand and want the traditional, idealized model of the child because that model cannot be supported by their experience or imagination.

The same is true of the traditional model of an adult. If one looks closely at the content of TV, one can find a fairly precise documentation not only of the rise of the "adultified" child but also of the rise of the "childified" adult. Television is as clear about this as almost anything else (although, without question, the best representation of the childlike adult is in the film *Being There,* which is, in fact, about the process I am describing). Laverne, Shirley, Archie, the crew of the Love Boat, the company of Three, Fonzie, Barney Miller's detectives, Rockford, Kojak, and the entire population of Fantasy Island can hardly be said to be adult characters, even after one has made allowances for the traditions of the formats in which they appear. With a few exceptions, adults on television do not take their work seriously (if they work at all), they do not nurture children, they have no politics, practice no religion, represent no tradition, have no foresight or serious plans, have no extended conversations, and in no circumstances allude to anything that is not familiar to an eight-year-old person.

Although students of mine who are dedicated TV watchers have urged me to modify the following statement, I can find only one fictional character regularly seen on commercial television, Felix Unger of *The Odd Couple,* who is depicted as having an adult's appetite for serious music and whose language suggests that he has, at one time in his life, actually read a book. Indeed, it is quite noticeable that the majority of adults on TV shows are depicted as functionally illiterate, not only in the sense that the content of book learning is absent from what they appear to know but also because of the absence of even the faintest signs of a contemplative habit of mind. (*The Odd Couple,* now seen only in reruns, ironically offers in Felix Unger not only an example of a literate person but a striking anomaly in his partner, Oscar Madison—a professional writer who is illiterate.)

A great deal has been written about the inanity of popular TV programs. But I am not here discussing that judgment. My point is that the model of an adult that is most often used on TV is that of the child, and that this pattern can be seen on almost every type of program. On game shows, for example, contestants are selected with great care to ensure that their tolerance for humiliation (by a simulated adult, the "emcee") is inexhaustible, their emotions instantly arousable, their interest in things a consuming passion. Indeed, a game show is a parody of sorts of a classroom in which childlike contestants are duly rewarded for obedience and precociousness but are otherwise subjected to all the indignities that are traditionally the schoolchild's burden. The absence of adult characters on soap operas, to take another example, is so marked that as of this writing a syndicated "teen-age" version of a soap opera, called *Young Lives,* has been embarked upon as if to document the idea that the world of the young is no different from the world of the adult. Here television is going one step further than the movies: *Young Lives* is *Bugsy Malone* without satire.

All of this is happening not only for reasons suggested in the last three chapters but also because TV tries to reflect prevailing values and styles. And in our current situation the values and styles of the child and those of the adult have tended to merge. One does not have to be a sociologist of the familiar to have noticed all of the following:

The children's clothing industry has undergone vast changes in the past decade, so that what was once unambiguously recognized as "children's" clothing has virtually disappeared. Twelve-year-old boys now wear three-piece suits to birthday parties, and sixty-year-old men wear jeans to birthday parties. Eleven-year-old girls wear high heels, and what was once a clear marker of youthful informality and energy, sneakers, now allegedly signifies the same for adults. The miniskirt, which was the most embarrassing example of adults mimicking a children's style of dress, is for the moment moribund, but in its place one can see on the streets of New York and San Francisco grown women wearing little white socks and imitation Mary Janes. The point is that we are now undergoing a reversal of a trend, begun in the sixteenth century, of identifying children through their manner of dress. As the concept of childhood diminishes, the symbolic markers of childhood diminish with it.

This process can be seen to occur not only in clothing but in eating habits as well. Junk food, once suited only to the undiscriminating palates and iron stomachs of the young, is now common fare for adults. This can be inferred from the commercials for McDonald's and Burger King, which make no age distinctions in their appeals. It can also be directly observed by simply attending to the distribution of children and adults who patronize such places. It would appear that adults consume at least as much junk food as do children.[4] This is no trivial point: it seems that many have forgotten when adults were supposed to have higher standards than children in their conception of what is and is not edible. Indeed, it was a mark of movement toward adulthood when a youngster showed an inclination to reject the kind of fare that gives the junk-food industry its name. I believe we can say rather firmly that this marker of the transition to adulthood is now completely obliterated.

There is no more obvious symptom of the merging of children's and adults' values and styles than what is happening with children's games, which is to say, they are disappearing. While I have found no studies that document the decline of unsupervised street games, their absence is noticeable enough and, in any case, can be inferred from the astonishing rise of such institutions as Little League baseball and Pee Wee football. Except for the inner city, where games are still under the control of the youths who play them, the games of American youth have become increasingly official, mock-professional, and extremely serious. According to the Little League Baseball Association, whose headquarters are in Williamsport, Pennsylvania, Little League baseball is the largest youth sports program in the world. More than fourteen hundred charters have been issued, over two and a half million youngsters participate, from ages six to eighteen. The structure of the organization is modeled on that of major league baseball, the character of the games themselves on the emotional style of big league sports: there is no fooling around, no peculiar rules invented to suit the moment, no protection from the judgments of spectators.

The idea that children's games are not the business of adults has clearly been rejected by Americans, who are insisting that even at age six, children play their games without spontaneity, under careful supervision, and at an intense competitive level. That many adults do not grasp the significance of this redefinition of children's play is revealed by a story that appeared in *The New York Times,* July 17, 1981. The occasion was a soccer tournament in Ontario, Canada, involving four thousand children from ten nations. In one game between ten-year-old boys from East Brunswick, New Jersey, and Burlington, Ontario, a brawl took place "after fathers had argued on the sidelines, players had traded charges of rough play and foul language, and one man from Burlington made a vulgar gesture." The brawl was highlighted by a confrontation be- tween the mothers of two players, one of whom kicked the other. Of course, much of this is standard stuff and has been duplicated many times by adults at "official" baseball and football games. (I have myself witnessed several forty-year-old men unmercifully "riding" an eleven-year-old shortstop be- cause he had made two errors in one inning.) But what is of most significance is the remark made by one of the mothers after the brawl. In trying to put the matter in perspective, she was quoted as saying, "It [the brawl] was just 30 seconds out of a beautiful tournament. The next night our boys lost, but it was a beautiful game. Parents were applauding kids from both teams. Over all, it was a beautiful experience." But the point is, What are the parents doing there in the first place? Why are four thousand children involved in a tournament? Why is East Brunswick, New Jersey, playing Burlington, Ontario? What are these children being trained for? The answer to all these questions is that children's play has become an adult preoccupation, it has become professionalized, it is no longer a world separate from the world of adults.

The entry of children into professional and world-class amateur sports is, of course, related to all of this. The 1979 Wimbledon tennis tournament, for example, was marked by the extraordinary performance of Tracy Austin, then not yet sixteen, the youngest player in the history of the tournament. In 1980, a fifteen-year-old player made her appearance. In 1981, a fourteen-year-old. An astonished John Newcombe, an old-time Wimbledon champion, expressed the view that in the near future twelve-year-old players may take the center court. But in this respect tennis lags behind other sports. Twelve-year-old swimmers, skaters, and gymnasts of world- class ability are commonplace. Why is this happening? The most obvious answer is that better coaching and training techniques have made it possible for children to attain adult-level competence. But the questions remain: Why should adults encourage this possibility? Why would anyone wish to deny children the freedom, informality, and joy of spontaneous play? Why submit children to the rigors of professional-style training, concentration, tension, media hype? The answer is the same as before: The traditional assumptions about the uniqueness of children are fast fading. What we have here is the emergence of the idea that play is not to be done for the sake of doing it but for some external purpose, such as renown, money, physical conditioning, upward mobility, national pride. For adults, play is serious business. As childhood disappears, so does the child's view of play.

This same tendency toward the merging of child and adult perspectives can be observed in their tastes in entertainment. To take an obvious example: The 1980 Nielsen Report on Television reveals that adults (defined as people over the age of eighteen) rated the following as among their fifteen most favored syndicated programs: *Family Feud, The Muppet Show, Hee Haw, M*A*S*H, Dance Fever, Happy Days Again,* and *Sha Na Na.* These programs were also listed among the top fifteen most favored by those between the ages of twelve and seventeen. And they also made the favored list of those between the ages of two and eleven! As for (the then) current shows, the male adult group indicated that *Taxi, Mork & Mindy, M*A*S*H, Three's Company, ABC Sunday Night Movie,* and *The Dukes of Hazzard* were among their favorites. The twelve-to-seventeen age group included the same shows.[5] In the 1981 Nielsen Report, adult males favored six syndicated programs (out of ten) that were the same as those favored by the twelve-to-seventeen age group, and four (out of ten) that were the same as the two-to-eleven age group.[6]

Such figures are painful to contemplate but are entirely consistent with the observation that what now amuses the child also amuses the adult. As I write, *Superman II, For Your*

Eyes Only, Raiders of the Lost Ark, and *Tarzan, the Ape Man* are attracting customers of all ages in almost unprecedented numbers. Twenty-five years ago, such films, which are essentially animated comic strips, would have been regarded as children's entertainment. Not as charming, innocent, or creative as, say, *Snow White and the Seven Dwarfs* but nonetheless clearly for a youthful audience. Today, no such distinctions need to be made. Neither is it necessary to distinguish between adult and youthful taste in music, as anyone who has visited an adult discotheque can attest. It is still probably true that the ten-year-old-to-seventeen-year-old group is more knowledgeable about the names and styles of rock groups than are those over the age of twenty-five, but as the declining market for both classical and popular "adult" music suggests, adults can no longer claim that their taste in music represents a higher level of sensitivity than teen-age music.[7]

As clothing, food, games, and entertainment move toward a homogeneity of style, so does language. It is extremely difficult to document this change except by repairing to anecdotes or by asking readers to refer to their own experience. We do know, of course, that the capacity of the young to achieve "grade level" competence in reading and writing is declining.[8] And we also know that their ability to reason and to make valid inferences is declining as well.[9] Such evidence is usually offered to document the general decline of literacy in the young. But it may also be brought forward to imply a decline of interest in language among adults; that is to say, after one has discussed the role of the media in producing a lowered state of language competence in the young, there is still room to discuss the indifference of parents, teachers, and other influential adults to the importance of language. We may even be permitted the assumption that adult control over language does not in most cases significantly surpass children's control over language. On television, on radio, in films, in commercial transactions, on the streets, even in the classroom, one does not notice that adults use language with more variety, depth, or precision than do children. In fact, it is a sort of documentation of this that there has emerged a small industry of books and newspaper columns that advise adults on how to talk as adults.

One may even go so far as to speculate that the language of the young is exerting more influence on adults than the other way around. Although the tendency to insert the word *like* after every four words still remains a distinctive adolescent pattern, in many other respects adults have found teen-age language attractive enough to incorporate in their own speech. I have recorded many instances of people over the age of thirty-five, and from every social class, uttering, without irony, such phrases as "I am into jogging," "Where are you coming from?" (to mean "What is your point of view?"), "Get off my case," and other teen-age locutions. I must leave it to readers to decide if this tendency is confirmed by their own experience. However, of one thing, I believe, we may be sure: Those adult language secrets to which we give the name "dirty words" are now not only fully known to the young (which may always have been the case) but are used by them as freely as they are by adults. Not only on the soccer field in Ontario but in all public places—ball parks, movie theaters, school yards, classrooms, department stores, restaurants—one can hear such words used comfortably and profusely even by children as young as six years old. This fact is significant because it is an example of the erosion of a traditional distinction between children and adults. It is also significant because it represents a loss in the concept of manners. Indeed, as language, clothing, taste, eating habits, etc., become increasingly homogenized, there is a corresponding decline in both the practice and meaning of civilité, which is rooted in the idea of social hierarchy.[10] In our present situation, adulthood has lost much of its authority and aura, and the idea of deference to one who is older has become ridiculous. That such a decline is in process can be inferred from the general disregard for rules and rituals of public assembly:

the increase in what are called "discipline problems" in school, the necessity of expanded security at public events, the intrusion of the loudest possible radio music on public space, the rarity of conventional expressions of courtesy such as "thank you" and "please."

All of the foregoing observations and inferences are, I believe, indicators of both the decline of childhood and a corresponding diminution in the character of adulthood. But there is also available a set of hard facts pointing to the same conclusion. For example, in the year 1950, in all of America, only 170 persons under the age of fifteen were arrested for what the FBI calls serious crimes, i.e., murder, forcible rape, robbery, and aggravated assault. This number represented .0004 percent of the under-fifteen population of America. In that same year, 94,784 persons fifteen years and older were arrested for serious crimes, representing .0860 percent of the population fifteen years and older. This means that in 1950, adults (defined here as those over and including fifteen years of age) committed serious crimes at a rate 215 times that of the rate of child crime. By 1960, adults committed serious crimes at a rate 8 times that of child crime; by 1979, the rate was 5.5 times. Does this mean that adult crime is declining? Not quite. In fact, adult crime is increasing, so that in 1979 more than 400,000 adults were arrested for serious crimes, representing .2430 percent of the adult population. This means that between 1950 and 1979, the rate of adult crime increased threefold. The fast-closing difference between the rates of adult and child crime is almost wholly accounted for by a staggering rise in child crime. Between 1950 and 1979, the rate of serious crimes committed by children increased 11,000 percent! The rate of nonserious child crimes (i.e., burglary, larceny, and auto theft) increased 8,300 percent.[11]

If America can be said to be drowning in a tidal wave of crime, then the wave has mostly been generated by our children. Crime, like most everything else, is no longer an exclusively adult activity, and readers do not need statistics to confirm this. Almost daily the press tells of arrests being made of children who, like those playing tennis at Wimbledon, are getting younger and younger. In New York City a nine-year-old boy tried to hold up a bank. In July 1981, police in Westchester County, New York, charged four boys with sexual assault of a seven-year-old girl. The alleged rapists were a thirteen-year-old, two eleven-year-olds, and a nine-year-old, the latter being the youngest person ever to be accused of first-degree rape in Westchester County.[12]

Ten- to thirteen-year-olds are involved in adult crime as never before. Indeed, the frequency of serious child crime has pushed youth crime codes to their limits. The first American juvenile court was established in 1899 in Illinois. The idea could come to its end before the century is out as legislators throughout the country hurriedly try to revise criminal laws so that youthful offenders can be treated as adults. In California a study group formed by the attorney general has recommended sending juveniles convicted of first-degree murder to prison rather than to the California Youth Authority. It has also recommended that violent offenders sixteen years old and younger be tried as adults, within the court's discretion.[13] In Vermont the arrest of two teen-agers in connection with the rape, torture, and killing of a twelve-year-old girl has driven the state legislature to propose hardening the juvenile codes.[14] In New York, children between the ages of thirteen and fifteen who are charged with serious crimes can now be tried in adult courts and, if convicted, can receive long prison terms. In Florida, Louisiana, New Jersey, South Carolina, and Tennessee, laws have been changed to make it easier to transfer children between the ages of thirteen and fifteen to adult criminal courts if the crime is serious enough. In Illinois, New Mexico, Oregon, and Utah, the privacy that usually surrounds the trials of juveniles has been eliminated: newspaper reporters may now regularly attend the proceedings.[15]

This unprecedented change in both the frequency and

brutality of child crime, as well as the legislative response to it, is no doubt attributable to multiple causes but none more cogent, I think, than that our concept of childhood is rapidly slipping from our grasp. Our children live in a society whose psychological and social contexts do not stress the differences between adults and children. As the adult world opens itself in every conceivable way to children, they will inevitably emulate adult criminal activity.

They will also participate in such activity as victims. Paralleling the assault on social order *by* children is the assault by adults *on* children. According to the National Center on Child Abuse and Neglect, there were 711,142 reported cases of child abuse in 1979. Assuming that a fair amount of child battering goes unreported, we may guess that well over two million instances of child abuse occurred that year. What can this mean other than that the special status, image, and aura of the child has been drastically diminished? It is only half an explanation to say that children are beaten up because they are small. The other half is that they are beaten up because they are not perceived as children. To the extent that children are viewed as unrealized, vulnerable, not in possession of a full measure of intellectual and emotional control, normal adults do not beat them as a response to conflict. Unless we assume that in all cases the adult attackers are psychopaths, we may conclude that at least part of the answer here is that many adults now have a different conception of what sort of a person a child is, a conception not unlike that which prevailed in the fourteenth century: that they are miniature adults.

This perception of children as miniature adults is reinforced by several trends besides criminal activity. For example, the increased level of sexual activity among children has been fairly well documented. Data presented by Catherine Chilman indicate that for young white females the rise has been especially sharp since the late 1960s.[16] Studies by Melvin Zelnick and John Kantner of The Johns Hopkins University conclude that the prevalence of sexual activity among never-married teen-age women, among all races, increased by 30 percent between 1971 and 1976, so that by age nineteen, 55 percent have had sexual intercourse.[17] We may safely assume that media have played an important role in the drive to erase differences between child and adult sexuality. Television, in particular, not only keeps the entire population in a condition of high sexual excitement but stresses a kind of egalitarianism of sexual fulfillment; sex is transformed from a dark and profound adult mystery to a product that is available to everyone—let us say, like mouthwash or underarm deodorant.

One of the consequences of this has been a rise in teen-age pregnancy. Births to teen-agers constituted 19 percent of all the births in America in 1975, an increase of 2 percent over the figure in 1966. But if one focuses on the childbearing rate among those of age fifteen to seventeen, one finds that *this is the only age group whose rate of childbearing increased in those years, and it increased 21.7 percent.*[18]

Another, and grimmer, consequence of adult-like sexual activity among children has been a steady increase in the extent to which youth are afflicted with venereal disease. Between 1956 and 1979, the percentage of ten-to-fourteen-year-olds suffering from gonorrhea increased almost threefold, from 17.7 per 100,000 population to 50.4. Roughly the same increase is found in the fifteen-to-nineteen-year-old group (from 415.7 per 100,000 to 1,211.4). The traditional restraints against youthful sexual activity cannot have great force in a society that does not, in fact, make a binding distinction between childhood and adulthood. And the same principle applies in the case of the consumption of drugs. For example, the National Institute on Alcohol Abuse and Alcoholism concludes that a substantial number of fifteen-year-olds drink "considerable amounts." In one study of the drinking habits of tenth-to-twelfth-graders, almost three times as many males indicated they were "heavier" drinkers (meaning they drink at least once a week and consume large amounts when they drink) than those who indicated they were "infrequent" drinkers (meaning they drink once a month at most and then in small amounts). Alcoholism, once considered an exclusively adult affliction, now looms as a reality for our new population of miniature adults. Of other drugs, such as marijuana, cocaine, and heroin, the evidence is conclusive: American youth consume as much of it as do adults.[19]

Such figures as these are unmistakable signs of the rise of the "adultified" child, but there are similar trends suggestive of the rise of the "childified" adult. For example, the emergence of the "old persons' home" as a major social institution in America bespeaks of a reluctance on the part of young adults to assume a full measure of responsibility for their parents. Caring for the elderly and integrating them into family life are apparently perceived as an intolerable burden and have rapidly diminished as adult imperatives. Perhaps more significant is the fact that the present generation of young adults is marrying at a dramatically lower rate and having fewer children than their parents' generation. Moreover, their marriages are not as durable. According to the National Center for Health Statistics, parents are getting divorced at twice the rate they did twenty years ago, and more children than ever before are involved in marital dissolution: 1.18 million in 1979 as compared to 562,000 in 1963. Although we must assume multiple causality for such a trend, including what Christopher Lasch calls the rise of the narcissistic personality, we may fairly claim that it indicates a precipitous falling off in the commitment of adults to the nurturing of children. The strongest argument against divorce has always been its psychological effect on children. It is now clear that more adults than ever do not regard this argument to be as compelling as their own need for psychological well-being. Perhaps we might even say that, increasingly, American adults want to be parents of children less than they want to be children themselves. In any case, children have responded to this new mood by, among other things, running away in droves. According to the FBI, 165,000 children were taken into custody by police in 1979.

It is assumed that at least three times that number went undetected.

In the face of all this one would expect the rise of a "philosophy" of sorts to justify the loss of childhood. Perhaps there is a principle governing social life that requires people to search for a way to affirm that which is inevitable. In any case, such a philosophy has, indeed, emerged, and we may take it as evidence of the reality it addresses. I refer here to what is sometimes called the Children's Rights Movement. This is a confusing designation, because under its banner are huddled two conceptions of childhood that are, in fact, opposed to each other. One of them, which I do *not* have in mind in these remarks, believes that childhood is desirable although fragile, and wishes to protect children from neglect and abuse. This view argues, for example, for the intervention of public authority when parental responsibility fails. This conception of childhood dates back to the nineteenth century and is simply a widening of the perspective that led to child labor laws, juvenile crime codes, and other humane protections. *The New York Times* has referred to those who stand up for this idea as "child savers."

The other conception of "child's rights" rejects adult supervision and control of children and provides a "philosophy" to justify the dissolution of childhood. It argues that the social category "children" is in itself an oppressive idea and that everything must be done to free the young from its restrictions. This view is, in fact, a much older one than the first, for its origins may be found in the Dark and Middle Ages when there were no "children" in the modern sense of the word.

As is frequently the case in such matters, we have here a "reactionary" position being advanced by those who think of themselves as "radicals." In any case, these are people who might be called "child liberators." Among the earliest of them was Ivan Illich, the brilliant social critic, whose influential book *Deschooling Society* (1971) argued against compulsory schooling not only on the grounds that schools were unimprovable but, even more, that compulsory schooling effectively bars the young from fully participating in the life of the community; that is, prevents them from being adults. Illich redefined the relationship of children to school by insisting that what most people see as a benevolent and nurturing institution is instead an unwarranted intrusion in the life and learning of a certain segment of the population. The force of Illich's argument derives from the fact that information is now so widely distributed, available from so many sources, and codified in ways that do not require sophisticated literacy that the school has lost much of its meaning as the fountainhead of learning. Moreover, as the distinction between childhood and adulthood becomes less marked, as children less and less have to *earn* adulthood, as less and less is there anything for them to *become,* the compulsory nature of schooling begins to appear arbitrary.

   This impression is intensified by the fact that educators have become confused about what they ought to be doing with children in school. Such ideas that one ought to be educated for the greater glory of God or Country, or even for the purpose of beating the Russians, lack both serious arguments and advocates, and many educators are willing to settle for what Marx himself would have emphatically rejected: education for entry into the marketplace. This being the case, a knowledge of history, literature, and art, which once was the mark of an educated adult, recedes in importance. Moreover, it is not as well established as many think that schooling makes an important difference in one's future earning power. Thus, the entire edifice of our educational structure is laced with dangerous cracks, and those who would demolish the structure altogether are by no means misinformed. Indeed, there is a sense in which their proposals are redundant. As childhood disappears, so must schools. Illich does not have to write a book about it so much as merely wait.

   All of this is the theme of John Holt's *Escape from Childhood.* In this and other books he argues for the liberation of the child from the constraints of a three-hundred-year-old tradition of bondage. His arguments are broadened—that is, taken to their logical conclusion—in Richard Farson's extraordinary book, *Birthrights* (1974). Farson argues that the child's right to information, to his or her own choice of education, to sexual freedom, to economic and political power, even to the right to choose his or her own home environment, must be restored at once. "We are not likely to err," he says, "in the direction of too much freedom."[20] Farson, who is not unaware of the history of childhood, evidently finds the fourteenth and fifteenth centuries a suitable model for the ways in which the young ought to be integrated into society. He believes, among other things, that the principal objection to incest is that people are made to feel unreasonably guilty about practicing it; that all sexual behavior should be decriminalized, including sex between adults and children; that arrangements need to be made to permit children to live wherever and with whom they wish, including "homes" governed by themselves; and that children must be given the right to vote "because adults do not have their interests at heart and do not vote in their behalf."[21]

Such a child's rights movement as this may be said to be a case of claiming that the disease is the cure. Expressed more neutrally, what this sort of advocacy represents, as noted, is an attempt to provide a rationalization for what appears to be an irreversible cultural tendency. Farson, in other words, is not the enemy of childhood. American culture is. But it is not a forthright enemy, in the sense that one might say, for example, that America is against communism. American culture does not *intend* to be against childhood. In fact, the language we use to talk about children still carries within it many of the assumptions about childhood that were established in the eighteenth and nineteenth centuries. Just as our language about war preserves the idea of a nineteenth-century war, when, in fact, such an idea today is preposterous, our language about children does not match our present social reality. For in a hundred years of redesigning how we communicate, what we communicate, and what we need to be in order to share in it all, we have reached the point of not needing children, just as we have reached the point (although we dare not admit it) of not needing the elderly. What makes Farson's proposals so horrifying is that without irony or regret he reveals the future.

Chapter 9

Six Questions

Having released myself early from the burden of offering "solutions" to the problem of the disappearance of childhood, I wish to conclude this book by putting forward several questions that readers may find of interest. Each of these questions occurred to me at some point in the course of my inquiry, and then attached itself, barnacle-like, to my mind. This is my way of getting free of them (at least for the moment), which is to say, I have tried to supply them with answers. To the extent that readers will have different answers, I shall be flattered to think the questions are important.

Was childhood discovered or invented?

This book begins with the statement that childhood is a social artifact, not a biological necessity. Readers who are well-versed in child psychology will regard this statement as, at best, problematic and, at worst, false. Backed by the authority of such researchers as Freud, Erik Erikson, Arnold Gesell, and, in particular, Jean Piaget, prevailing opinion holds that observable stages of child development are governed by biological imperatives. Indeed, Piaget calls his studies "genetic epistemology," by which he means that the child's advance from one level of intellectual achievement to the next follows a genetic principle. I have not gone into this matter because it is in most respects irrelevant to the issues discussed in this book. The fact is that the *idea of childhood as a social structure* did not exist in the Middle Ages, it arose in the sixteenth century, and is now disappearing. But, of course, if Piaget is right, then childhood was not invented by literacy but only discovered, and the new information environment is not "disappearing" it but only suppressing it.

I believe that Piaget's studies are limited by his essentially ahistorical approach. He gave insufficient attention to the possibility that the behaviors he observed in children might have been absent or at least quite different at earlier historical periods. Nonetheless, I rather hope that he is correct. If he is, we may encourage ourselves to believe that, given the slightest chance, childhood will assert itself, for, as it is said, you cannot fool Mother Nature, at least not forever. If, however, childhood is solely a creation of culture, as I am inclined to believe, then it would have to await a dramatic restructuring of our communication environment in order to reappear along strong and unmistakable lines. And this may never happen. We are thus faced with the possibility that childhood is a transitory aberration in cultural history, like the horse-drawn carriage or black scribbles on white paper.

To cheer myself up, I am willing to settle for the following formulation and hope that future research will confirm it: Childhood is analogous to language learning. It has a biological basis but cannot be realized unless a social environment triggers and nurtures it, that is, has need of it. If a culture is dominated by a medium that requires the segregation of the young in order that they learn unnatural, specialized, and complex skills and attitudes, then childhood, in one form or another, will emerge, articulate and indispensable. If the communication needs of a culture do not require the long-term segregation of the young, then childhood remains mute.

Does the decline of childhood signify a general decline of American culture?

America is the first and, at present, the only culture living entirely under the control of twentieth-century technology. With very few exceptions, Americans have been willing to accommodate their landscape, their cities, their business enterprises, their family life, and their minds to the requirements of what they choose to call "technological progress." Thus, we may rightly say that America is now in the midst of its Third Great Experiment, and the full results are by no means known.

The First Great Experiment, which Thomas Paine called "a revolution in the principles and practice of governments," began in the late eighteenth century, and posed the question, Is freedom of thought and expression a viable idea on which to base a political structure?" The Second Great Experiment, begun in the mid-nineteenth century, was of a social nature, and posed the question, Can a culture be forged out of a population made up of groups of people from all over the world, each with its own language, traditions, and habits? Granting certain failures along the way, we may say that both of these experiments have been successful and to a considerable extent have been the wonder and envy of the world.

The Third Great Experiment, begun at the start of this century, poses the question, Can a culture preserve humane values and create new ones by allowing modern technology the fullest possible authority to control its destiny? Aldous Huxley and George Orwell have already given their answer, and it is "No." Lewis Mumford has given his, and it is "Probably no," the same answer given by Norbert Wiener. Jacques Ellul gives his answer in almost yearly reports, and it is the most resounding "No" of all. Among those whose answer is some variety of "Yes" are Buckminster Fuller, Alvin Toffler, Melvin Kranzberg, Samuel Florman, and Isaac Asimov, the latter being positively giddy about both the accomplishments and the potential of technology. Obviously, the question is still open, and we are permitted to guess. That technology itself has been deified, that the political process has been degraded, that the adult mind has been diminished, and that childhood is waning are woeful signs. The world watches to see if America can survive the dismembering of its past, and then will make plans accordingly.

But America has not yet begun to *think*. The shock of twentieth-century technology numbed our brains and we are just beginning to notice the spiritual and social debris that our technology has strewn about us. But not everyone was dumbstruck. We may, for example, recall that Ralph Nader's *Unsafe at Any Speed,* published in 1965, was a powerful and popular critique of a major technology. It is true that it came *after* Americans had allowed the automobile to change their landscape, their cities, and their social life. But it came nonetheless. And it has been followed (and indeed was quietly preceded) by other critiques and maps of the path we have taken: McLuhan on *Understanding Media,* Ellul on *The Technological Society,* Wiener on *The Human Use of Human Beings,* Joseph Weisenbaum on *Computer Power and Human Reason,* Mumford on *The Myth of the Machine,* Kenneth Boulding on *The Meaning of the Twentieth Century,* Boorstin on *The Image,* to name a few. To the extent that such books, and others to come, will help to give Americans both pause and perspective, and suggest to them ways in which technology might serve their purposes (instead of the other way around), there is reason to hope that the early signs of cultural disintegration are not permanent.

As for childhood, I believe it must, in the long run, be a victim of what is happening. Electricity makes nonsense of the kind of information environment that gives rise to and nurtures childhood. But in losing childhood, we do not have to lose everything. After all, the printing press shattered the cohesion of a world religious community, destroyed the intimacy and poetry of the oral tradition, diminished regional loyalties, and created a cruelly impersonal industrial system. And yet, Western civilization survived with some of its humane values intact and was able to forge new ones, including those associated with the nurturing of children. Now that the first shock of what we have embarked upon is beginning to diminish, we may yet think ourselves into a more felicitous position and come out resembling something worth saving.

To what extent do the Moral Majority and other Fundamentalist groups contribute toward the preservation of childhood?

In the 1950s, as some elders will recall, if you ventured to observe that the Communist party had put forward a good idea on any subject, you had to prepare yourself for the accusation that you were, at best, a "fellow traveler," and, at worst, a card-carrying member of the party. In certain circles today the same sort of thinking prevails in respect to the Fundamentalist movement: to speak a word that coincides with any Fundamentalist position will earn you the accusation of having abandoned the liberal tradition. By way of preparation against that charge, I should say that the Fundamentalist revival is, in my opinion, potentially dangerous because it is infused with the spirit of religious bigotry and political authoritarianism. Moreover, I have the impression that many Fundamentalist Christians love their nation-state far more than they love their God, and that nothing makes them happier than that which would make their Lord despair: the addition of devastating new weapons to the nation-state's arsenal.

And yet, as previously noted, the Moral Majority, as they

are sometimes called, appears to me more aware of what the new information environment has done to children than any other group in the body politic. Its attempts to organize economic boycotts against sponsors of certain television programs, its attempts to restore a sense of inhibition and reverence to sexuality, its attempts at setting up schools that insist on rigorous standards of civilité, are examples of an active program aimed at preserving childhood. Of course, none of this can be effective in achieving that aim, since it is too little, comes too late, and does not, in fact, even address the problem of a completely restructured information environment. But I believe the effort is commendable nonetheless, and—who knows?—perhaps it may serve to slow down the dissolution of childhood so that we will have sufficient time to adjust to its absence.

The liberal tradition (or, as the Moral Majority contemptuously calls it, secular humanism) has had pitifully little to offer in this matter. For example, in opposing economic boycotts of TV sponsors, civil libertarians have taken the curious position that it is better to have Procter & Gamble's moral standards control television's content than Queen Victoria's. In any case, to the extent that a political philosophy can influence cultural change, the liberal tradition has tended to encourage the decline of childhood by its generous acceptance of all that is modern, and a corresponding hostility to anything that tries to "turn back the clock." But in some respects the clock is wrong, and the Moral Majority may serve as a reminder of a world that was once hospitable to children and felt deeply responsible for what they might become. It is permissible, I think, for those of us who disapprove of the arrogance of the Moral Majority to borrow some of their memories.

Are there any communication technologies that have the potential to sustain the need for childhood?

The only technology that has this capacity is the computer. In order to program a computer, one must, in essence, learn a language. This means that one must have control over complex analytical skills similar to those required of a fully literate person, and for which special training is required. Should it be deemed necessary that everyone must know how computers work, how they impose their special world-view, how they alter our definition of judgment—that is, should it be deemed necessary that there be universal computer literacy —it is conceivable that the schooling of the young will increase in importance and a youth culture different from adult culture might be sustained. But such a development would depend on many different factors. The potential effects of a medium can be rendered impotent by the uses to which the medium is put. For example, radio, by its nature, has the potential to amplify and celebrate the power and poetry of human speech, and there are parts of the world in which radio is used to do this. In America, partly as a result of competition with television, radio has become merely an adjunct of the music industry. And, as a consequence, sustained, articulate, and mature speech is almost entirely absent from the airwaves (with the magnificent exception of National Public Radio). Thus, it is not inevitable that the computer will be used to promote sequential, logical, and complex thought among the mass of people. There are, for example, economic and political interests that would be better served by allowing the bulk of a semiliterate population to entertain itself with the magic of visual computer games, to use and be used by computers without understanding. In this way the computer would remain mysterious and under the control of a bureaucratic elite. There would be no need to educate the young, and childhood could, without obstruction, continue on its journey to oblivion.

Are there any social institutions strong enough and committed enough to resist the decline of childhood?

There are only two institutions that have an interest in the matter. The first is the family; the other, the school. As already noted, the structure and authority of the family have been severely weakened as parents have lost control over the information environment of the young. Margaret Mead once referred to television, for example, as the Second Parent, by which she meant that our children literally spend more time with television than with their fathers. In such terms, fathers may be the Fourth or Fifth Parent, trailing behind television, records, radio, and movies. Indeed, encouraged by the trend toward the devaluation of parenthood, Bell Telephone has had the effrontery to urge fathers to use "Dial-a-Story" as a substitute for telling their own stories to children. In any case, it is quite clear that the media have diminished the role of the family in shaping the values and sensibilities of the young.

Moreover, and possibly as a result of the enlarged sovereignty of the media, many parents have lost confidence in their ability to raise children because they believe that the information and instincts they have about child-rearing are unreliable. As a consequence, they not only do not resist media influence, they turn to experts who are presumed to know what is best for children. Thus, psychologists, social workers, guidance counselors, teachers, and others representing an institutional point of view invade large areas of parental authority, mostly by invitation. What this means is that there is a loss in the intimacy, dependence, and loyalty that traditionally characterize the parent-child relationship. Indeed, it is now believed by some that the parent-child relationship is essentially neurotic, and that children are better served by institutions than by their families.

Even more devastating to the power of the family is the women's liberation movement. So that I am not misunderstood on this point, I must say at once that the liberation of women from limited social roles is one of the truly humane effects of the technological revolution and deserves the full support of enlightened people. But it cannot be denied that as women find their place in business, in the arts, in industry, and in the professions, there must be a serious decline in the strength and meaning of traditional patterns of child care. For whatever criticisms may be made of the exclusive role of women as nurturers, the fact is that it is women, and women alone, who have been the overseers of childhood, shaping it and protecting it. It is unlikely that men will assume anything like the role women have played, and still do, in raising children, no matter how sensible it might be for men to do so. Thus, as parents of both sexes make their way in the world, children become something of a burden, and, increasingly, it is deemed best that their childhood end as early as possible. All of this adds up to the fact that unless there occurs a 180° turn in social trends, the American family will not stand in strong opposition to the contraction and then dissolution of childhood.

As for school, it is the only public institution left to us based on the assumption that there are important differences between childhood and adulthood and that adults have things of value to teach children. For this reason, childlike optimists still write books advising educators on how they ought to conduct themselves, and, in particular, on how they might pursue conserving activities. But the declining authority of the schools has been well documented, and amid a radically changed communication structure they have become (to quote Marshall McLuhan) houses of detention rather than attention. Educators, of course, are confused about what they are ex-

pected to do with children. For example, as the teaching of
literacy becomes more difficult to do, educators are even losing their enthusiasm for that time-honored task and wonder
if it ought not be abandoned altogether. For another example,
equally depressing: In some schools, children as young as
eleven and twelve have inflicted upon them what is called
"career training," a clear symptom of the reemergence of the
miniature adult. It is evident that schools reflect social trends
far more powerfully than they can direct them, and are close
to impotent in opposing them.

Nonetheless, as a creation of literacy, the school will not
easily join in the assault on its parentage. In one form or
another, no matter how diluted the effort, the school will stand
as the last defense against the disappearance of childhood.

It goes without saying that in due course, when all teachers
and administrators are themselves products of the Television
Age, resistance will not only lose whatever strength it may
have had but its point will have been forgotten.

Is the individual powerless to resist what is happening?

The answer to this, in my opinion, is "No." But, as with
all resistance, there is a price to pay. Specifically, resistance
entails conceiving of parenting as an act of rebellion against
American culture. For example, for parents merely to remain
married is itself an act of disobedience and an insult to the
spirit of a throwaway culture in which continuity has little
value. It is also at least ninety percent un-American to remain
in close proximity to one's extended family so that children
can experience, daily, the meaning of kinship and the value
of deference and responsibility to elders. Similarly, to insist
that one's children learn the discipline of delayed gratification,
or modesty in their sexuality, or self-restraint in manners,
language, and style is to place oneself in opposition to almost
every social trend. Even further, to ensure that one's children

work hard at becoming literate is extraordinarily time-consuming and even expensive. But most rebellious of all is the attempt to control the media's access to one's children. There are, in fact, two ways to do this. The first is to limit the amount of exposure children have to media. The second is to monitor carefully what they *are* exposed to, and to provide them with a continuously running critique of the themes and values of the media's content. Both are very difficult to do and require a level of attention that most parents are not prepared to give to child-rearing.

Nonetheless, there are parents who are committed to doing all of these things, who are in effect defying the directives of their culture. Such parents are not only helping their children to *have* a childhood but are, at the same time, creating a sort of intellectual elite. Certainly in the short run the children who grow up in such homes will, as adults, be much favored by business, the professions, and the media themselves. What can we say of the long run? Only this: Those parents who resist the spirit of the age will contribute to what might be called the Monastery Effect, for they will help to keep alive a humane tradition. It is not conceivable that our culture will forget that it needs children. But it is halfway toward forgetting that children need childhood. Those who insist on remembering shall perform a noble service.

Notes

Introduction

1. Walzer, p. 358.
2. Plumb, p. 6.
3. Boorstin, *The Republic*, p. 64.

Chapter One

1. Cowley, p. 14.
2. According to Professor Lawrence Stone, director of Princeton University's Shelby Cullom Davis Center for Historical Studies, between 1971 and 1976 more than nine hundred important books and articles were published on the subject of the history of childhood and family life. By contrast, he points out, in the 1930s only about ten scholarly books and articles were published each year.
3. In *The Greek Way*, Edith Hamilton tells a legend about a Greek painter that suggests there would have been nothing unusual about painting a boy: A Greek painter exhibited a picture of a boy holding a bunch of grapes so lifelike that birds flew down to peck at them. When the painter was praised for being a master, he replied, "If I were, the boy would have kept the birds away." Miss Hamilton concludes from this legend that to the Greek mind nothing could be imagined to be as beautiful as the real. Grapes were to be painted to look like grapes, and boys to look like boys. But, in fact, we have

no such paintings of boys—assuming our meaning of the word—from the Greek world.

4. deMause, p. 26.
5. deMause, p. 40.
6. deMause, p. 16.
7. Plumb, p. 7.
8. Quoted in deMause, p. 45.
9. Elias, p. 182.
10. deMause, p. 28.
11. Havelock, *Origins,* p. 52.
12. Havelock, *Origins,* p. 65.
13. Havelock, *Origins,* p. 65.
14. Gimpel, p. 1.
15. Chaytor, p. 10.
16. Tuchman, p. 61.
17. Havelock, "Literate Communication," p. 91.
18. Tuchman, p. 53.
19. Plumb, p. 6.
20. Ariès, p. 20.
21. Ariès, p. 411.
22. Plumb, p. 6.
23. Plumb, p. 7.
24. This description is a paraphrase of Elias, p. 72.
25. Elias, p. 69.
26. deMause, p. 39.
27. Père de Dainville, as quoted in Ariès, p. 103.
28. Ariès, p. 103.
29. Ariès, p. 38.
30. Burke, p. 161.
31. Tucker, p. 231.
32. Pinchbeck and Hewitt, Vol. II, p. 300.
33. Tuchman goes on to say that women are mostly depicted as "flirts, bawds, and deceiving wives in the popular tales, saints and martyrs in the drama, unattainable objects of passionate and illicit love in the romances." Tuchman, pp. 50–51.
34. Tuchman, p. 50.
35. Ariès, p. 47.
36. Tuchman, p. 50.

Chapter Two

1. Eisenstein, p. 119.
2. As quoted by Eisenstein, pp. 121–22.

3. Eisenstein, p. 119.
4. For a full discussion of the various claims, see Butler, pp. 88–110.
5. As quoted in Steinberg, p. 19.
6. Gilmore, p. 186.
7. As summarized by James Carey, Dean, School of Communication, University of Illinois, in an unpublished essay, "Canadian Communication Theory: Extensions and Interpretations of Harold Innis."
8. From James Carey's unpublished essay, above.
9. For a detailed study of the effects of the stirrup on European social and economic organization, see Lynn White, Jr.'s *Medieval Technology and Social Change*.
10. White, p. 28.
11. Burke, p. 105.
12. McLuhan, p. 233.
13. Eisenstein, p. 230.
14. McLuhan, p. 233.
15. Eisenstein, p. 400.
16. Eisenstein, p. 233.
17. Even as late as the nineteenth century, the tradition of reading as training for public speaking was still extant. The aim of the McGuffey Readers, for example, was to train the ear more than the eye.
18. Lowenthal, p. 41.
19. Mumford, p. 136.
20. Pinchbeck and Hewitt, Vol. I, pp. 5–6.
21. Eisenstein, p. 78.
22. Barincou, p. 42.
23. Eisenstein, p. 105.
24. Eisenstein, pp. 103–4.
25. Eisenstein, p. 102.
26. As quoted in Eisenstein, p. 102.
27. Stone, "Educational Revolution," p. 43.
28. Stone, "Literacy and Education," pp. 76–77.

Chapter Three

1. Plumb, p. 9.
2. Mumford, p. 137.
3. Stone, "Literacy and Education," p. 71.
4. Stone, "Literacy and Education," p. 80.
5. Stone, "Literacy and Education," pp. 78–79.
6. Pinchbeck and Hewitt, Vol. I, p. 23.
7. Pinchbeck and Hewitt, Vol. I, pp. 23–24.
8. Stone, "Educational Revolution," p. 42.

9. Stone, "Educational Revolution," p. 42.
10. Stone, "Educational Revolution," p. 43.
11. Stone, "Literacy and Education," p. 99.
12. Stone, "Educational Revolution," p. 68.
13. Stone, "Literacy and Education," p. 74.
14. Pinchbeck and Hewitt, Vol. I, p. 42.
15. Plumb, p. 9.
16. Ariès, p. 188.
17. Ariès, p. 187.
18. Eisenstein, pp. 133–34.
19. Ariès, 57.
20. For a detailed discussion of the changing patterns of child-rearing in the seventeenth century, see Illick, pp. 303–50.
21. Pinchbeck and Hewitt, Vol. II, p. 299.
22. Ariès, p. 369.
23. Eisenstein, p. 133.
24. Du Boulay, pp. 90–91.
25. Eisenstein, p. 89.
26. Plumb, p. 9.
27. Quoted in Illick, pp. 316–17.
28. Elias, p. 179.
29. Ariès, p. 82.

Chapter Four

1. Stone, "Literacy and Education," p. 92.
2. Quoted in Pinchbeck and Hewitt, Vol. II, p. 354.
3. Pinchbeck and Hewitt, Vol. II, pp. 351–52.
4. Apparently this hideous practice was common both in England and on the Continent.
5. Stone, "Literacy and Education," p. 119.
6. Stone, "Literacy and Education," p. 90.
7. Stone, "Literacy and Education," p. 129.
8. For two penetrating examples of the nature of the attack on the family, see Donzelot and Lasch.
9. See deMause.
10. Ariès, p. 30.
11. For an interesting history of this organization, see Payne.
12. Excerpted from Wishy, p. 117.
13. Dewey, p. 55.

Chapter Five

1. There appears to be some dispute about whether or not Morse actually transmitted this question. Indeed, one authority claims that Morse's first public transmission expressed a quite different sentiment, his message being, "Attention Universe."

2. Quoted from *Dreadnaught Broadside,* a pamphlet produced by students at the University of Toronto.

3. See Boorstin, *The Image.*

4. For a fuller discussion of the epistemological biases of different forms of symbolization, see Langer, Salomon, or Postman (particularly the latter, pp. 47–70).

5. Arnheim, p. 195.

6. Heilbroner, p. 40.

7. Barthes, p. 91.

8. Strictly speaking, the Semitic "alphabet" was a syllabary and not a true alphabet, but the changeover to phonetic literacy was nonetheless a major event in the psychological history of Western culture.

9. See Taylor's *The History of the Alphabet* for a detailed discussion of the evolution of phonetic literacy.

10. See Havelock's *Origins of Western Literacy* for a discussion of this point.

11. From a chapter in an unpublished book by Reginald Damerall of the University of Massachusetts.

12. Readers who are interested in the behavior of young children should consult the studies of Daniel R. Anderson, Department of Psychology, University of Massachusetts.

13. Mankiewicz and Swerdlow, p. 17.

Chapter Six

1. See Boorstin's *The Image* for his development of the idea of the pseudo-event.

2. See the Singers and Zuckerman's *Teaching Television.*

3. It is, of course, possible through government intervention to control television and thereby control the kind of information it will make accessible. Indeed, in most countries in the world that is exactly the case. But wherever and whenever television programming is free of rigid government restrictions, the American pattern is followed.

4. For an excellent treatment of how television makes available "back region" information, see Joshua Meyrowitz's *No Sense of Place: A Theory on the Impact of Electronic Media on Social Structure and*

Behavior, unpublished doctoral dissertation, New York University, 1978.

5. If one is willing to accept the current metaphors of genetics, then, of course, the question of who will be a male and who a female is also determined by information, i.e., genetic information.

6. Mead, p. 64.

7. See "Sexual Portrayals Using Children Legal Unless Obscene, Court Rules," *The New York Times,* May 13, 1981, p. 1.

8. Bettelheim, p. 4.

9. As quoted in Mead, p. 64.

Chapter Seven

1. See Bernstein's review in *The Dial,* Vol. 2, No. 6 (June 1981), pp. 46–49.

2. As quoted in *Backstage,* June 19, 1981, p. 60.

3. As quoted in *The Des Moines Register,* June 15, 1981, p. 7c.

Chapter Eight

1. See Leonide Martin's *Health Care of Women,* p. 95. However, this widely held belief has been challenged by Vern L. Bullough of the State University of New York at Buffalo. See "Drop in Average Age for Girls' Maturing Is Found to Be Slight," *The New York Times,* July 11, 1981, p. 17.

2. See George Masnick and Mary Jo Bane's *The Nation's Families: 1960–1990* for documentation of the decline of household members and the rise of the single-member household.

3. For documentation and analysis of the decline of the Disney empire, see "Wishing Upon a Falling Star at Disney," *The New York Times Magazine,* November 16, 1980.

4. McDonald's insists on keeping private its figures as to how much of its food different age groups consume. The best I could get from them is the statement that young adults with small children are the largest group among those who patronize McDonald's. The categories McDonald's inventories are small children, "tweens," teens, young adults, and seniors.

5. These figures are from *Nielsen Report on Television 1980.*

6. *Nielsen Report on Television 1981.* Both this report and the 1980 report are available upon request to A. C. Nielsen Company, Nielsen Plaza, Northbrook, Illinois 60062.

7. According to RCA, the largest producer of classical music recordings, in the early 1960s the company released approximately eight new

recordings a month. Today, that figure is down to four. A spokesman for RCA claims this situation is similar for every other company in the business. RCA also concedes that there has been a steady decline in the share of the market of both classical music and sophisticated popular music. Today, classical music, opera, and chamber music account for about seven percent of all sales. The rest is mostly rock, country, and jazz.

8. Among the many studies documenting this decline is one conducted by the California Department of Education in 1979. Seniors tested under the California Assessment Program continued to perform (as they had in 1978) sixteen percentage points below what the testing industry says is the national average for reading.

9. In a report released in 1981, the National Assessment of Educational Progress revealed that the inferential reasoning of thirteen-year-olds declined throughout the period of the 1970s.

10. For an excellent historical analysis of these relationships, see Sennett's *The Fall of Public Man.*

11. These figures were compiled by using the 1950 and 1970 Uniform Crime Report (published by the FBI) and the 1950 and 1970 census.

12. See the New York *Daily News,* July 17, 1981, p. 5.

13. See the United Press International report of June 22, 1981.

14. See the New York *Daily News,* July 17, 1981, p. 5.

15. For a comprehensive review of the changing attitudes toward child crime, see *The New York Times,* July 24, 1981.

16. Cited in Melvin Zelnik and John Kantner's "Sexual and Contraceptive Experience of Young Unmarried Women in the United States, 1976 and 1971," *Family Planning Perspectives,* Vol. 9, No. 2 (March/April 1977), pp. 55–58.

17. See Zelnik and Kantner, above.

18. See Stephanie Ventura's "Teenage Childbearing: United States, 1966–75," *The Monthly Vital Statistics Report,* a publication of the National Center for Health Statistics.

19. See "Student Drug Use in America, 1975–1980," prepared by Lloyd Johnson, Jerald Bachman, and Patrick O'Malley of the University of Michigan Institute for Social Research. It is available from the National Institute on Drug Abuse, Rockville, Maryland 20857.

20. Farson, p. 153.

21. Farson, p. 179.

Bibliography

Ariès, Philippe. *Centuries of Childhood,* trans. by Robert Baldrick. New York: Random House, Vintage Books, 1962.

Arnheim, Rudolf. *Film As Art.* Berkeley: University of California Press, 1957.

Barincou, Edmond. *Machiavelli.* Westport, Conn.: Greenwood Press, 1975.

Barthes, Roland. *Mythologies,* trans. by Annette Lavers. New York: Hill & Wang, 1977.

Bettelheim, Bruno. *The Uses of Enchantment: The Meaning and Importance of Fairy Tales.* New York: Alfred A. Knopf, 1976.

Boorstin, Daniel J. *The Image.* New York: Harper & Row, Colophon Books, 1961.

———. *The Republic of Technology.* New York: Harper & Row, 1978.

Burke, James. *Connections.* Boston: Little, Brown & Company, 1978.

Butler, Pierce. *Origin of Printing in Europe.* Chicago: University of Chicago Press, 1940.

Chaytor, H. J. *From Script to Print.* Cambridge, England: The University Press, 1945.

Cowley, Robert. "Their Work Is Child's Play." *Horizon,* Vol. 13, No. 1, Winter 1971.

deMause, Lloyd. "The Evolution of Childhood," in Lloyd deMause, ed., *The History of Childhood.* New York: The Psychohistory Press, 1974.

Dewey, John. *The School and Society.* Chicago: University of Chicago Press, 1899.

Donzelot, Jacques. *The Policing of the Family.* New York: Pantheon Books, 1979.

Du Boulay, F.R.H. *An Age of Ambition: English Society in the Late Middle Ages.* New York: Viking Press, 1970.

Eisenstein, Elizabeth. *The Printing Press As an Agent of Change.* Cambridge, England: Cambridge University Press, 1979.

Elias, Norbert. *The Civilizing Process: The History of Manners.* New York: Urizen Books, 1978.

Farson, Richard. *Birthrights.* New York: Macmillan, 1974.

Gilmore, Myron. *The World of Humanism.* New York: Harper & Brothers, 1952.

Gimpel, Jean. *The Medieval Machine.* New York: Holt, Rinehart & Winston, 1976.

Havelock, Eric. *Origins of Western Literacy.* Toronto: Ontario Institute for Studies in Education, 1976.

————. "The Coming of Literate Communication to Western Culture." *Journal of Communication,* Winter 1980.

Heilbroner, Robert. "The Demand for the Supply Side." *The New York Review of Books,* Vol. 28, No. 10, June 11, 1981.

Holt, John. *Escape from Childhood.* New York: Ballantine Books, 1976.

Illick, Joseph. "Child Rearing in Seventeenth Century England and America," in Lloyd deMause, ed., *The History of Childhood.* New York: The Psychohistory Press, 1974.

Langer, Susanne K. *Feeling and Form.* New York: Charles Scribner's Sons, 1953.

Lasch, Christopher. *Haven in a Heartless World: The Family Besieged*. New York: Basic Books, 1977.

Lowenthal, Leo. *Literature and the Image of Man*. Boston: Beacon Press, 1957.

Mankiewicz, Frank, and Joel Swerdlow. *Remote Control*. New York: Ballantine Books, 1979.

Martin, Leonide. *Health Care of Women*. New York: J. B. Lippincott Company, 1978.

Masnick, George, and Mary Jo Bane. *The Nation's Families: 1960–1990*. Boston: Auburn House, 1980.

McLuhan, Marshall. *The Gutenberg Galaxy: The Making of Typographic Man*. Toronto: University of Toronto Press, 1962.

Mead, Margaret. *Culture and Commitment: A Study of the Generation Gap*. Garden City, N.Y.: Doubleday & Co., 1970.

Mumford, Lewis. *Technics and Civilization*. New York: Harcourt, Brace & World, 1934.

Payne, George Henry. *The Child in Human Progress*. New York and London: G. P. Putnam's Sons, 1916.

Pinchbeck, Ivy, and Margaret Hewitt. *Children in English Society, Volume I: From Tudor Times to the Eighteenth Century*. Toronto: University of Toronto Press, 1969.

————. *Children in English Society, Volume II: From the Eighteenth Century to the Children Act of 1948*. Toronto: University of Toronto Press, 1973.

Plumb, J. H. "The Great Change in Children." *Horizon*, Vol. 13, No. 1, Winter 1971.

Postman, Neil. *Teaching As a Conserving Activity*. New York: Delacorte Press, 1979.

Salomon, Gavriel. *The Interaction of Media, Cognition, and Learning*. San Francisco: Jossey-Bass, 1979.

Sennett, Richard. *The Fall of Public Man*. New York: Random House, Vintage Books, 1978.

Singer, Dorothy G., Jerome L. Singer, and Diana M. Zuckerman. *Teaching Television: How to Use TV to Your Child's Advantage*. New York: The Dial Press, 1981.

Steinberg, Sigfrid H. *Five Hundred Years of Printing.* Baltimore: Penguin Books, 1974.

Stone, Lawrence. "The Educational Revolution in England, 1500–1640." *Past and Present,* No. 28, July 1964.

————. "Literacy and Education in England, 1640–1900." *Past and Present,* No. 42, February 1969.

Taylor, Isaac. *The History of the Alphabet.* New York: E. P. Dutton & Co., 1974.

Tuchman, Barbara W. *A Distant Mirror.* New York: Alfred A. Knopf, 1978.

Tucker, M. J. "The Child as Beginning and End: Fifteenth and Sixteenth Century English Childhood," in Lloyd deMause, ed., *The History of Childhood.* New York: The Psychohistory Press, 1974.

Walzer, John F. "A Period of Ambivalence: Eighteenth-Century American Childhood," in Lloyd deMause, ed., *The History of Childhood.* New York: The Psychohistory Press, 1974.

White, Lynn, Jr. *Medieval Technology and Social Change.* London: Clarendon Press, 1962.

Wishy, Bernard. *The Child and the Republic.* Philadelphia: University of Pennsylvania Press, 1968.

Index

BOOKS BY NEIL POSTMAN

"No contemporary essayist writing about American pop culture is more fun to read and more on target."
—Los Angeles Times

CONSCIENTIOUS OBJECTIONS
STIRRING UP TROUBLE ABOUT LANGUAGE, TECHNOLOGY AND EDUCATION

In a series of feisty and ultimately hopeful essays, one of America's sharpest social critics casts a shrewd eye over contemporary culture to reveal the worst—and the best—of our habits of discourse, tendencies in education, and obsessions with technological novelty.

"Postman uses cogent arguments, sharp needles and gentle humor to challenge readers to change their ways of thinking...delightful." *—St. Louis Post-Dispatch*

Current Affairs/Science/Education/0-679-73421-X

TECHNOPOLY
THE SURRENDER OF CULTURE TO TECHNOLOGY

Neil Postman chronicles our transformation from a society that uses technology to one that is shaped by it, as he traces its effects upon what we mean by politics, intellect, religion, history—even privacy and truth.

"A provocative book...a tool for fighting back against the tools that run our lives." *—Dallas Morning News*

Current Affairs/Sociology/0-679-74540-8

VINTAGE BOOKS

AVAILABLE AT YOUR LOCAL BOOKSTORE, OR CALL TOLL-FREE
TO ORDER: 1-800-733-3000 (CREDIT CARDS ONLY)